79

FAMILY

...ter Sauce flavored with Lemon

...egg yolks flavored with lemon juice,
... to make a thick, yellow, creamy
... and is often the most
... extremely easy
... recipe

ROSALIND CREASY'S

Recipes From the Garden

200 Exciting Recipes from the author of

The Complete Book of Edible Landscaping

TUTTLE PUBLISHING
Tokyo • Rutland, Vermont • Singapore

Disclaimer: Edible flowers are wonderful additions to just about any dish. Some flowers are poisonous, however, so it is essential to confirm that any flowers you intend to use for culinary purposes are of a nonpoisonous variety that is safe to eat. It is also crucial that these flowers have not been treated with chemical sprays. Throughout this cookbook, you'll find many recipes that call for edible flowers. To be sure that you have correctly identified ones that you intend to use, refer to a field guide to edible plants or consult an expert. And remember, common names are not reliable; use Latin names for positive identification of plants and flowers. Never use flowers from a florist shop in your recipes—they will have been sprayed with chemicals not appropriate for consumption. The author and publisher cannot be held responsible for any illness or injury caused by using inedible flowers in these recipes.

Acknowledgments: Special thanks to Gudrun Riter for all her help in testing the recipes and food styling these photographs. Thanks, as well, to Carole Saville for help with the food styling.

Published by Tuttle Publishing, an imprint of Periplus Editions (HK) Ltd., with editorial offices at 364 Innovation Drive, North Clarendon, Vermont 05759 U.S.A.

Text and photos copyright © 2008 Rosalind Creasy

Library of Congress Cataloging-in-Publication Data
Creasy, Rosalind
  Rosalind Creasy's recipes from the garden / Rosalind Creasy. — 1st ed.
      208 p.: col. ill.; 29 cm.
  Includes index.
  ISBN 978-0-8048-3768-2 (hardcover)
1. Cookery (Vegetables) 2. Cookery (Herbs) 3. Cookery (Flowers) I. Title. II. Title:
Recipes from the garden.
  TX801.C74 2008
  641.6'51—dc22   2007031187

Paperback Edition ISBN 978-0-8048-4105-4

Distributed by
North America, Latin America & Europe
Tuttle Publishing, 364 Innovation Drive
North Clarendon, VT 05759-9436 U.S.A.
Tel: 1 (802) 773-8930, Fax: 1 (802) 773-6993
info@tuttlepublishing.com
www.tuttlepublishing.com

Asia Pacific
Berkeley Books Pte. Ltd.
61 Tai Seng Avenue #02-12
Singapore 534167
Tel: (65) 6280-1330, Fax: (65) 6280-6290
inquiries@periplus.com.sg
www.periplus.com

First edition
13 12 11 10 09   7 6 5 4 3 2 1

Printed in Singapore

Contents

The Gardening Chef
—an evolution of american eating

Ho-hum cardboard tomatoes, astringent green bell peppers, and bland, store-bought food—that's how most of America ate a generation or two ago. Where were they hiding the luscious rainbow of heirloom tomatoes? Why weren't green peppers allowed to ripen to their sweet natural red—much less yellow or orange? And why were cilantro, fresh basil, mâche, and radicchio kept out of the mainstream? Somehow we got on the wrong track, no longer knowing where our food came from or what was in season. We're now reclaiming our culinary birthright—one deeply connected to the Earth—through home gardening, shopping at farmers' markets, and eating local foods.

Throughout my life, gardening and cooking have played major roles. In looking back, it seems that my personal experiences can shed some light on the changes that have been happening in American cuisine during the past 50 years.

My adventures began when I was five years old and my father deeded me my first vegetable garden—a little plot adjacent to his big garden in my hometown of Needham, Massachusetts. There I grew offshoots from his strawberry plants, extra tomato and bean seedlings, and lots of flowers. I saw it as an extension of my dollhouse and continually moved the plants around. I don't remember ever harvesting anything from my garden, but that didn't matter because I was having a great time experimenting with plants while enjoying my father's company.

Over the years, he taught me through example what I later realized were some important links between the kitchen and garden: putting the water on to boil before picking the corn, judging when an asparagus spear is at its peak, and harvesting string beans and partially stringing them at the same time. (Use your thumbnail to cut part way through the bean below the stem and pull the bean down and away. This leaves the "stem-y" top and the string from one side of the bean hanging on the vine. I now use the same technique with snap peas.)

My mother was the cook in our house. Looking back, I must say that she wasn't very inspired—bless her heart. It was the 1950s, after all. Although she made great roasts and steaks, she boiled most vegetables. Because they were garden fresh and she usually didn't overcook them, her vegetable dishes were pleasant. But Mom's repertoire was very limited. She baked or boiled potatoes; it probably never occurred to her to roast, sauté, or grill them—or any other vegetable for that matter. The only herbs she used were in poultry seasoning

Left: The home gardener's harvest allows for fast, delicious, and healthy meals made from nature's freshest and finest. Here is a salad of ornamental kale, curly endive, and Batavian lettuce, ready for garnishing with pansies, one of the most commonly used varieties of edible flower. **Following page:** This harvest of traditional Italian vegetables features eggplants, red and yellow tomatoes, leeks, peppers, and squash blossoms.

for the holidays, and those were dried and came in a tin. She certainly never prepared anything that was remotely spicy.

After I married, my husband Robert and I set up housekeeping in Cambridge, Massachusetts. In retrospect, I can't believe my luck. Cambridge in the early 1960s was home to both Julia Child and Joyce Chen, the doyennes of cooking in America. The town was abuzz with food mania. Both women had written popular cookbooks and Julia had her landmark cooking show— what inspirations they were! Robert, being a clever, food-loving man with a sophisticated palate, came up with great birthday presents for me. The first was the gastronomic bible of the day, Julia Child's *Mastering the Art of French Cooking* (written with Louisette Bertholle and Simone Beck), followed the next year by the *Joyce Chen Cookbook*. Living in the city, my gardening days were temporarily over, but I can't think of better introductions to the techniques for creating some of the world's best food.

I was home with one baby, then a second, so for well over five years I cooked my way through both books. From Julia, I learned to make hollandaise for my asparagus; to put together what was then an exotic dish with eggplant and zucchini—ratatouille; to serve homemade squash soup in a hollowed-out pumpkin; and to make Pommes Anna, a crisp cake of thin potato slices layered with butter. Over the years, I also learned how to make a good chicken stock, blanch vegetables, and even make French bread.

Years later, I gave a slide presentation on edible landscaping to Julia Child and members of the American Institute of Wine and Food. I brought along my dog-eared copy of *French Cooking* for her to sign. When she saw it, she hugged it, saying that such a well-worn copy was the ultimate compliment. Before she signed my book, she ran her hand over the pages, feeling the splatters and wrinkles, and read some of my hand-written notes: "Robert loved it!" "Make this again and add more herbs," and "Freezes well."

Although I never had the good luck to meet her, Joyce Chen was no less vital to my culinary journey. Growing up, my only exposure to Chinese food was the not-so-authentic, and not-so-thrilling, canned chop suey with chow mein noodles—clearly a poor take on one of the world's most sophisticated cuisines. Although I'd had Joyce Chen's cookbook for many months, I hadn't used it. Apparently Robert noticed, and so decided to take me to Joyce's restaurant. What a culinary awakening that was! The flavors were complex yet easy to like. Inspired by the meal, I was ready to delve into the cookbook. From it, I learned how to make wonton soup, cook rice properly, and stir-fry (not to mention the importance of having all the vegetables and seasonings completely prepared before starting to cook). Compared to French cooking, Chinese techniques were more straightforward. I soon discovered that Chinese dishes were easier to make for everyday meals than Julia's fancy French recipes. They also fit better into our limited budget and seemed healthier (using oil instead of butter, less meat, and amounting to far fewer calories). My friends and I started to go to Boston's Chinatown to seek out pak choi, pea pods, fresh ginger, and Chinese cabbage—all new to me. Even though we lived in an apartment, I also got back into gardening in a very small way: I grew bean sprouts in my kitchen. They were tasty in my stir-fries—nothing like the slimy ones in canned chop suey—and they were lots of fun and easy to grow.

My return to gardening was made complete in 1968 when we moved to the San Francisco Bay area. We bought a ranch-style house in Los Altos on a small lot with a sunny front yard and a very shady backyard. My gardening

opportunities were still limited, because vegetables and fruits need lots of sun and the concept of ripping out the front lawn and replacing it with an edible garden had not yet occurred to me. For a few years a friend and I shared her wonderful vegetable garden; we planted the usual rows of corn, beans, tomatoes, basil, peppers, and both summer and winter squash. It was great to once again enjoy luscious homegrown tomatoes and to start the water boiling before we picked the corn. Right in front of our eyes—and to our great surprise—we found the green bell peppers ripening to a rich red. Who knew?

Robert and I acclimated well to California and loved all the ethnic foods that were so readily available. These exciting new dishes were influencing my cooking, so I decided that it was time to have a small garden area of my own where I could experiment with some of the more unusual edible plants required to make them. I transformed the parking strip in front of the lawn into a flower border, into which I snuck a few spicy peppers for chili rellños, jalapeños for tacos, lots of basil for pesto, cilantro for stir fries, tarragon for Julia's béarnaise sauce, and artichokes, which, as it turns out, were the stars of the "flower border" because they were so beautiful.

In the mid 70s, I decided to go back to school to get a degree in horticulture with the goal of becoming a landscape designer. About the same time, Robert started overseeing scientific projects all over the world for IBM. I got to go along with him to places like Milan, Grenoble, Cairo, Taipei, Paris, Hong Kong, and Vienna. While he was working with clients in each city, I would head out to the markets and the gardens. Often, a host spouse would translate for me when I stood puzzled in front of a large pile of unusual-looking radicchios or chili peppers. My most frequent questions were "How do you cook it?" and "Where can I get seeds?" During dinner I usually shared my wonder at all the great vegetables and herbs I was discovering. Our hosts would tell me more about them, and if I was lucky, they shared recipes.

In France, it was eye opening not to have traditional potato salad with mayonnaise but instead a *salade niçoise* with fingerling potatoes, *haricots verts*, and fresh seared tuna with tarragon vinaigrette. The braised baby bok choi and mushrooms in spicy ginger sauce in Hong Kong, and Italy's slivers of raw artichoke bedecked with curls of Parmesan cheese and drizzled with lemon juice and olive oil blew the top off my perception of vegetables. This started me down the road to growing even more fantastic edible plants, or tracking them down in the market. When harvest time came, I'd use the recipes I had saved or develop my own.

I was fortunate to have firsthand experience of so many unusual foods. In the 60s when I started cooking, there were few recipes available using any but the most common of vegetables and herbs. The two books my husband had gifted to me were exceptions, yet I was still held back by the limited availability of interesting ingredients. In fact, there was an unwritten rule in the cookbook-publishing world: "Never use an ingredient the average cook could not find in his or her local grocery store." Consequently, American cooking allowed little room for innovation and imploded in on itself. It was not until the early 1980s when Julee Rosso and Sheila Lukins agreed to write their soon-to-be-classic *The Silver Palate Cookbook*—and insisted on including "exotic" ingredients like fresh basil and mangos—that this rule changed. Creative ingredients began to show up in a flood of good eating.

Meanwhile, gardening was running a parallel path to cooking. In the mid-twentieth century, the seed industry limited in the name of efficiency vegetable and herb varieties available to the home gardener. There were color standards:

Thanks to America's broadening culinary horizons, it is now possible for chefs living in even the remotest of locations to purchase or grow once-rare edibles. This brightly colored taco, for example, is made with yellow tomatoes, 'Ruby Queen' corn, and orange bell peppers.

green for snap beans and bell peppers, red for tomatoes, orange for carrots, and brown skin with white flesh for potatoes. Purple—beans, peppers, tomatoes, carrots and potatoes—was nowhere to be seen, and neither were any other bright colors. Agriculture and America's general lack of interest in vegetables and herbs had joined to present a united front against anything but run-of-the-mill garden produce. But exciting and flavorful edibles were on the horizon.

The next step on my own gardening journey came during a trip to a kibbutz outside Haifa, Israel, where I was struck by how hard it was for the Israelis to grow food on the limited arable land in their country, which is mostly desert. I was convinced that Americans were wasting the valuable soil around their homes, and that they should use it to grow at least some of their own vegetables and fruits. Thus, my version of edible landscaping was born. With this inspiration, I got to work on what would become *The Complete Book of Edible Landscaping*, which Sierra Club Books published in 1982. To my surprise, it became a big hit.

Great rumblings had been occurring in the cooking world and were continuing. And here I was—once again—at the epicenter of one of the quake zones—Northern California. In the 70s, the flower children pushed us toward healthier foods, including many Asian specialties and vegetables. Alice Water's Berkeley restaurant, Chez Panisse, which featured local and beautifully prepared seasonal foods, was becoming a phenomenon. Greens Restaurant opened in 1979 in San Francisco led by Deborah Madison (then chef), and became one of the premier vegetarian restaurants in the nation. Greens formed a close bond with Green Gulch, a large organic garden. Farmers' markets in California were opening at an exponential rate and more and more chefs and gardeners began to work together. In nearby Napa Valley, the wine and cheese industries were taking off. Many of these businesses gave cooking demonstrations out of their gardens. At about the same time, CCOF (California Certified Organic Farmers) was busy trying to develop organic standards for vegetables and fruits. And the world sat up and took notice.

In 1985, in the midst of this glorious food revolution, I signed a contract to begin working on my second book, *Cooking from the Garden*. Unlike my previous book, this one was going to be all about how to grow ethnic foods, baby greens, edible flowers, and heirloom vegetables—and how to cook them in unique and interesting ways. I needed a trial garden to test at least a hundred different varieties of vegetables at one time, simultaneously growing a dozen tomato varieties, twenty different types of lettuce, and so on. These were vegetables that few cooks or gardeners had seen, such as green or striped tomatoes and red-hearted radishes, and I was faced with not only the challenge of growing them, but also creating recipes that showcased their unique flavors and textures. The only suitable place for such a garden was my sunny front yard. And I now had the skills to make it beautiful!

I hired Wendy Krupnick, an experienced food gardener, for this gargantuan two-year project. She dug up the entire front yard, transforming it into a succession of garden beds. I kept copious notes throughout the process: from finding and obtaining seeds, growing them out, photographing the resulting plants at the peak of their glory, harvesting them, and finally on to cooking, eating, and photographing the delectable results. Just as I hoped, we grew out hundreds of wonderful edibles in mini-gardens

Right: Many international dishes that were once unusual have become staples of the American diet. This classic Italian minestrone soup is a delightful opportunity to showcase homegrown vegetables. **Following page:** Heirloom dishes such as this rhubarb-strawberry cobbler are irresistible and delicious American traditions.

with Mexican, French, German, Asian, Native American, herb, and salad themes. It may be hard to fathom now, but back then there was almost no information on growing or cooking with foods out of the American mainstream; there was no Internet. We were pioneers, learning about roasting vegetables, how to preserve their colors when cooking them, where to find chipotle peppers, and discovering the world of Middle Eastern cookery. Even something that is familiar now, such as balsamic vinegar, was hard to find; salsa was exotic, even though in America today it is more widely used as a condiment than ketchup.

I was truly blessed in this endeavor; Wendy was not only an expert gardener, but had also worked in a number of restaurants (including Chez Panisse). She brought sophistication to my recipes. In addition, Wendy was the state secretary for CCOF; organic farmers from all over the state came to meetings at my house. They shared new research in organic gardening methods, often bringing unusual or special produce to "show and tell" and giving us cutting-edge recipes and ideas.

I also came to be an early supporter of the Seed Savers Exchange, and felt an urgent need to help preserve some of the thousands of heirloom vegetable varieties that were going extinct. I could do my part by singing their praises to the public and food professionals. And with my ever-changing garden, I found that I had the means to make a difference.

After I finished my book, the *Los Angeles Times* asked me to write a monthly syndicated column about unusual vegetables. Since I couldn't buy broccoli raab, Japanese eggplant, lemon thyme, Vietnamese coriander, tomatillos, or the many other edibles I wanted to write about, I had to grow them in my garden (and go through the familiar process of planting, note-taking, photographing, recipe testing, and so on). Once again, we grew a variety of gardens, with each bed embracing a different theme, and to distinguish them from the ones in my soon-to-be-published book, we created formal brick paths and built an arbor spanning the main walkway.

By the following year when the book finally came out, there was more media demand for new and varied gardens, including television coverage on *CNN Headline News* (a story about heirloom vegetables) and *CBS This Morning* (a feature on growing a front yard garden of mesclun salad greens). The *New York Times* did a feature article on cooking with unusual vegetables, and used their own photographer. Within a year, I became a contributing editor at *Country Living Gardener* magazine, and I needed even more new recipes and photos from my garden. Clearly, I was off on a new career path.

Since I started planting the front yard garden more than twenty years ago, my succession of gardeners and I have changed it out and planted new edibles of every sort twice a year, which means I've had more than forty trial gardens. It's been great fun finding a range of unique themes. For instance, in 1992 (the 500th anniversary of Columbus's landing in the New World), I planned a garden full of indigenous plants including the "three sisters" (beans, corn, and squash, a trio of companionable plants that Native Americans traditionally grew together), tomatoes, chili peppers, sunflowers, and amaranths. I've planted and cooked from at least a dozen distinctive salad gardens—some in containers and many combined with edible flowers. My spice garden included the herbs which, when they go to seed, are considered spices (anise, coriander, cumin, dill, and fennel), along with a patch of unusual mustards for seed—brown, white, and black.

There has been an Italian wild greens garden, a salsa garden, a grain garden, and a rainbow vegetable garden featuring everything from blue potatoes to rainbow chard, red carrots, and purple artichokes.

Recipes from the Garden is a compilation of some of my favorite dishes; it's my way to share the innumerable culinary adventures I've had through decades of cooking from my garden. Along the way I've had the privilege of meeting many cooks who garden and gardeners who cook—professionals and amateurs alike—who have been gracious enough to share their recipes.

This book is not meant to be an A to Z primer on vegetables and herbs. Instead, it is a collection of recipes that follows my meandering journey through a garden of Eden that you, too, can enjoy—whether the ingredients come from your garden, a grocery store, or the local farmers' market.

You'll find here enticing recipes that are flavorful, packed with nutrition, and generally light on saturated fats and sodium. I have included a vast range of recipes from easy to complex, suitable for beginners and long-time cooks:

- **Easy and quick recipes using familiar ingredients:** Mint Whipped Cream, Tomato and Basil Salad, and Baked Beets
- **Dishes that are amazingly nutritious, and filled with vitamins and antioxidants:** Classic Minestrone Soup; Hearty Greens with Pears, Blue Cheese, and Chives; and Oriana's Cabbage Salad
- **Recipes sure to please:** Crab and Asparagus Salad with Fancy Greens and Sorrel Dressing, Tortilla Soup, Pork Shoulder Sandwiches with Tomatillos
- **Gifts from the garden:** Rosemary Pesto, Basil in Parmesan, and Dried Tomatoes
- **Edible flower recipes:** Chive Blossom Butter, Lavender Sugar, and Flower Confetti Salad
- **Old-fashioned classics with a modern twist:** Baked Apples with Dried Cherries and Hazelnuts, Corn Pudding, and Rhubarb-strawberry Cobbler
- **Show-off recipes for devoted garden cooks:** Red Cherry Peppers Roasted and Stuffed with Mozzarella Cheese and Prosciutto, Deep-fried Squash Blossoms with Chili Cream, and Garden Celebration Salad
- **Memorable desserts:** Rose Petal Sorbet, Golden Chard Dessert Tart, and Carrot Pie

Even if you don't have your own garden, you, too, can create most of the recipes in this book. With each passing day, more and more ingredients that were once considered exotic are becoming accessible. No doubt some of these recipes will bring out your adventurous spirit and tempt you to sample from our new global buffet. As you look through the recipes in this book, you will find yourself planning your next meal, as well as next season's garden—from sorrel and Cinderella pumpkins to cherry peppers and nasturtiums, from melons to fava beans.

As Julia Child would say, "Bon appétit!"—and happy gardening.

Rosalind Creasy
Los Altos, California

Herb blends,
salad dressings,
and more

Fresh herb blends

The French are fond of herbs, and starting with a few French classics is a lovely way to begin this book. *Bouquet garni* and *fines herbes* are such versatile herb mixes, we've all probably used variations without calling them by their official titles.

Bouquet Garni

Bouquet garni is used to infuse a soup, stock, or sauce with complex flavors. Herbs are tied together with aromatic vegetables, added at the beginning of cooking, and removed at the end.

1 small leek, or large leek sliced lengthwise, white part only
1 carrot
2 celery ribs, with greens
1 sprig fresh lovage or 4 tablespoons celery leaves
3 sprigs fresh parsley
3 sprigs fresh thyme
1 bay leaf

Tie all the ingredients together with clean white string. Leave a tail on the string so you can secure it to the pot and remove it easily.

Fines Herbes

Fines herbes is a mixture of chopped herbs. You will see dried mixes labeled "fines herbes," but the elusive flavors of the primary herbs—tarragon, parsley, and chervil—fade when dried. The traditional mixture calls for equal amounts of minced fresh parsley, tarragon, chervil, and chives or thyme. This mix is added at the last minute to soups, sauces, vinaigrettes, and savory egg dishes.

Gremolata

Here's another traditional herb blend—this one from Italy. It adds a "wallop" of flavor when sprinkled over osso buco, roast lamb, baked chicken, and fish; when added to soups before serving; or when stirred into marinades and sauces.

1 large lemon
$^1/_2$ cup (15 g) chopped fresh Italian parsley
1 small garlic clove, minced
$^1/_8$ teaspoon salt
Dash of freshly ground black pepper

Grate the lemon peel. Place it in a small bowl, and mix in the parsley, garlic, salt, and pepper. It will keep for three days in the refrigerator. Makes $^2/_3$ cup (20 g).

Left: Salad greens can be grown in beds or containers, as shown here. **Right:** These are the workhorses of the herb garden: flat-leaf and curly parsley, sage, rosemary, and French and lemon thyme. Use them in butters, pasta sauces, salad dressings, soups, stuffings, meat stews, and in a marinade for roast meats.

Even a garden with only a few herb plants produces enough to share. Before a party, gather up little bouquets of fresh herbs, tie them with raffia, and give them to your host or hostess. Or dry herbs and give them as a bridal shower gift. For a festive presentation, put the dry herbs in a basket and add a great bottle of olive oil, a fancy vinegar, and your favorite salad dressing recipe.

Salad herb blends

A basic green salad can be given many faces by changing the selection of fresh herbs. Here are a number of fresh herb salad blends.

Tangy Herb Blend

This blend is wonderful over a large salad of mixed lettuces and tomatoes with a basic vinaigrette.

12 to 16 fresh sorrel leaves, chopped
2 tablespoons chopped fresh parsley
3 tablespoons fresh burnet leaves

Asian Herb Blend

This herb mix can be used in a salad—try making the vinaigrette with rice wine vinegar and a little soy sauce, and add grilled scallops to the salad. This blend can also be added to a stir-fry at the end of cooking.

2 tablespoons chopped fresh cilantro
2 teaspoons minced fresh lemongrass

1 tablespoon finely snipped fresh
   Oriental chives

Classic Mesclun Herb Blend

Mesclun salad mixes are great from the garden and are now available in many markets. Traditionally, fresh herbs are included in the salad. Add the following herb blend to your mesclun next time and see what you think.

2 tablespoons chopped fresh chervil
1 tablespoon chopped fresh thyme
1 tablespoon chopped fresh tarragon

Fresh Flavor Herb Blend

Another herb variation adds dimension to vegetable salads. Try it on

tomatoes and cucumbers, with avocados and root vegetables, or added to risotto.

1 tablespoon snipped fresh dill
2 teaspoons chopped fresh borage
1 tablespoon snipped fresh chives

Summer Essence Herb Blend

Use the following blend in tomato soup, on pizza, in a green or bean salad, or in just about any dish with lots of tomatoes.

2 tablespoons chopped fresh basil
2 teaspoons chopped fresh tarragon
1 tablespoon chopped fresh parsley

Dry herb blends

Drying herbs not only preserves the flavor for the off-season but sometimes can enhance the flavor as well. Many of the following blends have many variations under the same name, such as the classic *herbes de Provence*.

Herbes de Provence

In looking through French reference books, I found many different herb blends that were called herbes de Provence. The ones I gravitated toward were from Jacques Pépin, chef, author, and TV series host, and Antoine Bouterin, chef/owner of Bouterin in New York City. Other chefs add savory or sweet marjoram to the blend. According to Pépin, his blend is equal parts dried thyme, sage, rosemary, lavender, and fennel seeds. Use the blend with red meats and vegetables.

Herbes de Provence à la Bouterin

4 tablespoons dried thyme
2 tablespoons dried rosemary
1 tablespoon dried lavender
1 tablespoon fennel seeds
3 bay leaves, crushed

Tex-Mex Hot Barbecue Blend

A blend from a spicy part of the world, this mixture is great rubbed on beef, chicken, and pork before barbecuing. This recipe is for the "hot-heads"; if you don't like your food blazing, omit the chile Piquín.

2 tablespoons crumbled, dried Mexican oregano
1 tablespoon cumin seeds, toasted and ground
1 teaspoon chile Piquín flakes
1 teaspoon chili powder

Fresh Light Blend

Use this blend for poultry stuffing, in a lemon butter over fish, and added to soups.

2 tablespoons dried lemon thyme
1 tablespoon dried rosemary
1 tablespoon dried Greek oregano

Roast Potato Blend

2 tablespoons dried sweet marjoram
2 tablespoons dried thyme

For a delicious potato dish, parboil approximately 24 small potatoes (or 1½ lbs/650 g) until almost tender. Put them in a shallow baking pan with 3 tablespoons of olive oil, and stir to coat. Sprinkle salt and pepper and the herb blend over them and stir again. Bake at 400°F (200°C), stirring occasionally until golden brown (Bake about 20 to 30 minutes.)

Roasted Root Vegetable Blend

Here's another roasting mix; you can use it interchangeably with the Roast Potato Blend.

1 tablespoon dried rosemary
½ tablespoon dried savory
½ tablespoon dried thyme

Salad dressings

The dressing we all need in our repertoire is the basic vinaigrette. This ageless combination of ingredients is elegant in its simplicity, and its quality depends on superior ingredients. Once the basic vinaigrette is mastered, it has endless variations. And then there all those wonderful creamy dressings—some are made with yogurt, others with cheese, cream, or buttermilk. They are also valuable in the salad repertoire. Newcomers to the dressing world are low-fat and nonfat ones. Salads are so much a part of a healthy diet that it makes sense to lower the caloric content for day-to-day salads. With the help of a lot of talented cooks, we now have an ever-expanding choice of tasty low-calorie dressings.

Basic Vinaigrette

Though the proportions of ingredients in a basic vinaigrette differ from cook to cook, the following is a representative recipe. It makes enough to dress a salad for four to six people. As vinaigrettes keep well for a few days, I generally double the amounts to make enough for two salads, refrigerating half.

1½ to 2 tablespoons wine vinegar
½ teaspoon salt
Dash of freshly ground black pepper
5 to 6 tablespoons extra-virgin olive oil

Mix the vinegar, salt, and pepper and with a whisk blend in the oil to taste. Drizzle most of the dressing over 4 to 6 handfuls of mixed greens, toss gently, and taste. Add more dressing, if needed, and serve.

Vinaigrette with Blood Oranges and Champagne Vinegar

Created by Annie Somerville, executive chef at Greens restaurant in San Francisco, this sophisticated dressing is delicious.

½ teaspoon finely minced orange
   zest
2 tablespoons freshly squeezed
   blood orange or tangelo juice
1 tablespoon champagne vinegar
¼ teaspoon salt
3 tablespoons extra-virgin olive oil

In a small bowl, whisk together the orange zest, juice, vinegar, and salt. Once the salt dissolves, whisk in the oil. *Makes ⅓ cup (85 ml).*

Asian Vinaigrette

Asian greens seem to cry out for their own dressing. I like to use a basic vinaigrette but substitute Asian ingredients and seasonings to complement the "cabbagy" flavor. This rich (but very low-cal) and flavorful vinaigrette is perfect on all sorts of mixed Asian greens. I love to sprinkle a teaspoon or so of toasted sesame seeds over the salad after it is dressed, to accentuate the flavors. You can add all sorts of steamed vegetables to the salad. You may also add cooked chicken as well.

½ teaspoon honey
¼ teaspoon freshly grated ginger
1½ tablespoons rice wine vinegar
2 tablespoons commercial low- or
   nonfat defatted chicken or vegetable stock
½ teaspoon tamari or soy sauce
½ teaspoon chili oil
1 tablespoon cold-pressed toasted
   sesame oil
1 tablespoon fresh chopped cilantro
   (optional)

In a small bowl, mix the honey and ginger. Slowly add the vinegar, whisking it in to incorporate the honey. Slowly add the stock, whisking it in. Add the tamari and oils and stir to blend. *Makes ½ cup (125 ml).*

Vegetable Marinade

Vinaigrettes don't always need to be used as a dressing drizzled over a salad; they can also be used to marinate vegetables that are then served cold, by themselves or over greens. Chef John Downey, from Downey's in Santa Barbara, California, likes to use a vinaigrette filled with lots of

garden-fresh herbs to marinate lightly cooked vegetables for appetizer salads. This light combination of olive and corn oils and cider vinegar lets the flavors of the greens and herbs predominate. The recipe makes enough to use as a marinade or to dress two or three green salads.

¼ cup (65 ml) cider or wine vinegar
1 to 3 teaspoons high-quality mustard
1 to 2 tablespoons minced shallots,
   dried, or scallions (green onions),
   garlic, or a combination of all three
⅓ cup (10 g) finely chopped fresh
   herbs such as basil, dill, fennel,
   parsley, or thyme
Salt and freshly ground black pepper
1 cup (250 ml) oil

In a bowl, combine all the ingredients except the oil or process them briefly in a food processor. Slowly whisk in the oil or add it to the processor. Let the mixture stand for ½ hour to allow the flavors to blend; check the seasoning. Refrigerate the unused portion and use within a few days. *Makes 1½ cups (350 ml).*

Creamy salad dressings

Creamy dressings are at their best served with crunchy, crisp lettuces and with assertive greens. As a rule they are not used with baby greens, because they weigh down the greens and overpower the delicate flavors.

Garden Ranch Dressing

This creamy dressing is great on all types of lettuces and mixed greens. Beets and croutons would be great additions to the salad. This recipe makes enough for at least two large salads and will keep in the refrigerator for up to ten days.

- **1 tablespoon grated shallots or sweet onion**
- **1 garlic clove, minced or pressed**
- **1 cup (250 ml) buttermilk**
- **$^1/_2$ cup (125 ml) mayonnaise**
- **1 teaspoon honey**
- **1 teaspoon white wine vinegar**
- **$^1/_4$ teaspoon hot sauce**
- **$^1/_4$ teaspoon salt**
- **$^1/_4$ teaspoon freshly ground black pepper**
- **1 tablespoon finely chopped fresh parsley**
- **1 tablespoon finely chopped fresh chives**
- **1 teaspoon chopped fresh thyme**
- **1 teaspoon chopped fresh chervil**
- **$^1/_2$ teaspoon chopped fresh tarragon**

In a mixing bowl, combine all the ingredients, blending them together well. Refrigerate before serving. *Makes 1$^1/_2$ cups (350 ml).*

Light Roquefort Dressing

No dressing made with Roquefort can be truly low-cal; however, this version cuts out much of the fat but not the flavor of the classic version. You can also substitute Gorgonzola or Maytag blue cheese, one of the few domestic blue cheeses that works in this recipe. The dressing keeps for up to ten days in the refrigerator.

- **1 garlic clove, minced or pressed**
- **1 tablespoon lemon juice**
- **1 tablespoon extra-virgin olive oil**
- **4 oz (125 g) Roquefort cheese, crumbled**
- **$^1/_3$ cup (85 g) nonfat plain yogurt**
- **$^2/_3$ cup (170 g) low-fat sour cream**
- **3 tablespoons nonfat milk**
- **$^1/_4$ teaspoon hot sauce**
- **$^1/_4$ teaspoon salt**
- **$^1/_4$ teaspoon freshly ground black pepper**

In a small mixing bowl, blend the garlic, lemon juice, oil, and Roquefort with a fork until creamy. Add the yogurt, sour cream, milk, hot sauce, and salt and pepper. Whisk until the mixture is well blended. Refrigerate until ready to serve. *Makes 2 cups (475 ml).*

Sauce Verte

Here is a variation of the classic French *sauce verte* and the German *grüne sosse* traditionally served over cold cooked vegetables. It can also be used as a dip for cooked or raw vegetables.

- **$^1/_2$ cup (115 g) fresh blanched and drained spinach**
- **$^1/_4$ cup (25 g) chopped fresh watercress leaves or $^1/_8$ cup (15 g) fresh young arugula (rocket) or nasturtium leaves**
- **$^1/_4$ cup (10 g) fresh chopped parsley leaves (preferably Italian)**
- **4 tablespoons fresh chopped sorrel leaves**
- **1 scallion (green onion) or 1 shallot or 2 tablespoons snipped chives**
- **1 small garlic clove, crushed**
- **2 tablespoons minced fresh tarragon, dill, or chervil**
- **1$^1/_2$ cups (350 ml) mayonnaise**
- **$^1/_2$ cup (125 g) sour cream or yogurt**

Blend all the ingredients in a blender or food processor. *Makes about 2$^1/_2$ cups (625 ml).*

Salads come in many different styles. Here is a large garden salad, a Caesar salad, and a composed salad of cucumbers and yellow tomatoes. Even the simplest of salads can be a celebration of flavor, with a little imagination and the addition of fresh herbs and homemade dressing.

Low-calorie dressings

There are many ways to cut down on fat and calories in salad dressings. Most of their calories come from the oil, which gives them a rich flavor and a slippery "mouth feel." You can still get the same effect by using less oil and adding vegetable or chicken stock. The amount you substitute is a matter of personal taste. I've given proportions I like; you may want more or less oil. You can also use a little maple syrup or honey for the oil, to help add viscosity. To add rich flavors to a dressing, try adding fruit juice or tomato juice or substitute some of the richer-flavored nut oils for a milder olive or vegetable oil. The Asian Vinaigrette (page 25) is one such recipe; here are a few more.

Basic Low-Cal Vinaigrette

This dressing is to my salad repertoire what my jeans are to my wardrobe. Always there, always comfortable. It's at home with any mixed or mesclun salad, and I often substitute my favorite herb of the day for the fennel.

3 tablespoons commercial low- or
   nonfat chicken stock
1 tablespoon fresh lemon juice
1 1/2 tablespoons extra-virgin olive oil
1 teaspoon chopped fresh fennel or
   chives, basil, dill, or tarragon
1/8 teaspoon salt
1/8 teaspoon freshly ground black
   pepper

Pour all the ingredients into a small bowl and whisk to blend them. Use immediately or refrigerate for up to a week. *Makes 1/2 cup (125 ml).*

Sun-Dried Tomato Dressing

I met David Hirsch, chef at the Moosewood Restaurant in Ithaca, New York, and author of *The Moosewood Restaurant Kitchen Garden*, while visiting the restaurant. I asked him if he'd share a salad dressing recipe that was low in fat. David suggests serving this robust thick and creamy dressing with greens "that are more than delicate," such as crunchy romaine, endive, arugula (rocket), radicchio, lightly steamed vegetables, and potatoes. The dressing looks best when made with sun-dried tomatoes that have retained some of their red color. The carrots also add color as well as sweetness, fiber, and nutrition.

5 dry-packed sun-dried tomatoes
1/3 cup (50 g) raw grated carrot
1 garlic clove, minced or pressed
2 tablespoons extra-virgin olive oil

1 1/2 to 2 tablespoons cider vinegar
1 tablespoon minced fresh parsley
1 1/2 tablespoons minced fresh basil

Soak the tomatoes in boiling water to cover for about 15 minutes, or until they're soft. Drain the tomatoes, reserving 2 tablespoons of the liquid. Combine all the ingredients except the fresh herbs in a blender, add 1/3 cup (85 ml) water and the reserved 2 tablespoons of drained water, and purée until smooth. Stir in the herbs. *Makes 1 cup (250 ml).*

Jody's Low-Cal French Dressing

So-called French dressing is actually an American invention. This dressing is also flavored with tomatoes, but the result is very different. Jody Main contributed this recipe. On some days she is my venerable garden manager, on others she caters healthy food to conscientious companies or tests products for a natural-food store. This dressing keeps in the refrigerator for about a week.

1 cup (250 ml) tomato juice
1/4 cup (55 g) tomato paste
Juice of 1 lemon
1 teaspoon honey
1 garlic clove, pressed
1/4 teaspoon freshly ground black
   pepper
1 teaspoon grated onion
2 tablespoons red wine vinegar

Combine the ingredients by rotating them in a jar with a good seal, or whisk them together in a small bowl. *Makes 1 1/2 cups (350 ml).*

Salads are a perfect, tasty way to enjoy the bounty of a home garden. Here are peppers, tomatoes, garlic, and green beans—all great additions to any salad.

Flower butters can turn a snack into a surprising treat for guests. This rose butter is presented garnished with whole rose petals.

Flower butters

Both savory and sweet butters can be made with flowers. Probably the most versatile savory butters are made from chive blossoms or nasturtium flowers. Serve these savory butters with a crisp French bread or melt them over vegetables, fish, or poultry. Or also add savory herbs, lemon juice, or other flavorings such as ground chipotle peppers or grated fresh ginger. Sweet flower butters can be made with roses, violets, lavender, and pineapple sage and are a treat on egg breads, sugar cookies, or as a mystery filling between layers of pound or sponge cake. Not all edible flowers are equally tasty. Before you prepare the blossoms taste a few petals to make sure they please your palate.

Nasturtium Butter

4 oz (125 g) unsalted butter (1 stick), room temperature
12 to 18 nasturtium flowers
2 to 4 fresh nasturtium leaves, or a few sprigs of fresh parsley
3 or 4 chive leaves (optional)

Chive Blossom Butter

4 oz (125 g) unsalted butter (1 stick), room temperature
10 to 12 large, barely open common chive flowers, florets (petal clusters) separated
2 small sprigs of fresh parsley, or 8 or 10 large chive leaves

Rose Butter

4 oz (125 g) unsalted butter (1 stick), room temperature
1 teaspoon superfine sugar, or finely granulated sugar (sometimes called baker's sugar)
$1/4$ teaspoon almond extract
Generous handful of organic rose petals from the fragrant old-fashioned types, such as 'Belle of Portugal,' any of the rugosa roses and damasks, and the 'Eglantine' rose (enough to yield 2 tablespoons of chopped petals)

Making any flower butter involves the same process. First, remove the petals from the flowers and wash them well in cold water—check for critters. Gently pat them dry in a towel or dry them in a salad spinner. Using a very sharp knife, mince the flowers and any leaves. (Mincing is easier if you roll the blossoms into a small ball before cutting them.) Cut a stick of room-temperature butter into 6 or 8 pieces and then mash them with a fork. When the butter is fairly soft, slowly incorporate any flavorings and the flowers and leaves. With a rubber spatula put the mixture into a small butter crock or decorative bowl. Refrigerate until serving time. Flower butters can be frozen in sealed containers for 2 months.

All three recipes make a little more than $1/2$ cup (125 g).

Asian condiments

Asian cuisines are widely varied, but one thing many of them share is a fondness for pickled vegetables. These vegetables add a flavorful kick to meals and may be served either as stand-alone condiments or incorporated into stir-fries and other dishes. Pickling can be a particularly useful technique for gardeners and local food enthusiasts, as it can extend the life of plentiful crops.

Pickled Daikon and Carrots

My neighbor Helen Chang and friend Mai Truong have helped me make these pickles. Pickling daikon in this manner is traditional in many parts of Asia. In China, these pickles might be part of a farmer's lunch, served with rice and a vegetable stir-fry. In Vietnam, showing the influence of the French, the slices might be used in a sandwich with liverwurst, head cheese, and herbs, or served with noodles and fragrant herbs. In Japan, they would be part of a selection of pickles offered as condiments at a meal.

If you prefer a crisp pickle, parboil the daikon and carrots in a quart of boiling water into which ½ teaspoon of alum has been added. See the Pickled Mustard recipe on the following page for more information on the use of alum.

1 lb (500 g) white daikon radish (12–16 in/30–40 cm long, 2 in/5 cm in diameter)
1 medium carrot
2 teaspoons salt
½-in (13-mm) slice fresh ginger root
½ cup (125 ml) rice wine vinegar
½ cup (115 g) sugar

Peel the daikon and carrots and cut them into ¼ x 3-inch (6 mm x 7.5-cm) matchstick strips. Put the vegetables in a medium bowl and sprinkle the salt over them. Crush the ginger slice with the back of a cleaver and add it to the vegetables. Stir the daikon and carrots with your hands to disperse the salt evenly. Set the bowl aside and let it sit at room temperature for 1 hour.

Drain the vegetables and then, using your hands, gently squeeze them to remove more of the liquid. Add the vinegar and sugar to the vegetables and stir until thoroughly mixed. Set aside to marinate at room temperature for 2 hours. Remove the ginger and discard it. Put the pickled vegetables in a tight-sealing container and refrigerate until use.

These pickles keep refrigerated for up to 2 weeks.

Pickled Ginger

Pickled ginger is most popular in Japan, where it invariably accompanies sushi and sashimi. The commercially prepared pickles often have added red food coloring but traditionally it is colored with red shiso leaves (perilla) as it is here.

¼ lb (125 g) young ginger root
¼ cup (65 ml) rice vinegar
2 tablespoons mirin
2 tablespoons sake
2 tablespoons sugar
6 red shiso (perilla) leaves

In a small saucepan, bring the rice vinegar, mirin, sake, and sugar to a gentle boil. Stir until the sugar dissolves. Cool the liquid.

Bring a small pot of water to a boil. Brush the ginger under running water, slice thinly, and then blanch slices for 1 minute. Drain the ginger and then transfer it into a sterilized half-pint canning jar, layering it evenly with the whole shiso leaves. Pour the cooled liquid over the ginger. Cover and let marry for 3 days in the refrigerator

before serving. The ginger will keep in the refrigerator for up to 1 month. *Makes ½ pint (250 ml).*

Pickled Mustard Cabbage

Pickled mustard cabbage is a staple in much of Asia. Mai Truong helped me make it the way her Vietnamese mother taught her. Small amounts of the mustard are used to add flavor to stir-fries. It can be eaten over rice for a simple meal, or enjoyed as a condiment. Alum is used to make the pickle crunchier and to retain some of the green color but it is not a critical ingredient. You can get alum at pharmacies and Asian grocery stores. If you can't make your own, you can buy pickled mustard in the refrigerated section of most Asian markets.

3 quarts (3 liters) water
½ cup (150 g) kosher salt
4 cups (800 g) sugar
2 large Chinese mustards (look for solid-hearted varieties such as Amsoi)

1 teaspoon solid alum or ½ teaspoon powdered alum

Bring the water to a boil; add the salt and sugar. Stir until the salt and sugar have dissolved. Cool the liquid to room temperature.

Wash the mustard and cut a slit a few inches deep in the large base so the pickling liquid can penetrate the flesh. In a large pot, bring about 4 quarts (4 liters) of water to a rolling boil. Add the alum. Blanch the mustard for about 30 seconds. Drain and cool the mustard to room temperature.

Put the mustard into a large plastic container that can be sealed. Pour the pickling liquid over the mustard; make sure the entire surface is submerged. (If you don't have enough, make up more pickling liquid and add it.) Put the mustard in a cool, dark place to pickle for a week. The pickled mustard keeps in the refrigerator for a few weeks. *Makes 6 cups (725 g) or about 1½ pounds.*

Above: Pickled ginger, a Japanese staple
Left: Chinese mustard cabbage, before and after pickling **Far left:** Pickled daikon and carrots, ready for serving

Italian fundamentals

This section includes information about preparing and enjoying some of Italy's most fundamental and flexible foods. Because Italian cuisine is elegant and simple, it is especially important to begin with the freshest and best of ingredients—like the vegetables, herbs, and fruits from your own garden or local farmers' market.

Roasted Pimientos

Use these peppers to add zing to your sandwiches, soups, pasta dishes, and sauces.

Approximately 12 large pimiento peppers
8 garlic cloves
³/₄ to 1 cup (190–250 ml) extra-virgin olive oil

Roast the peppers under the broiler or on the grill until blackened but not cooked through, peel them, and remove the seeds and stem ends. Layer the peppers in a quart jar with a good seal.

Lightly crush the garlic cloves with the back of a chef's knife. In a small frying pan, heat the oil and slowly sauté the garlic over low heat for about 5 minutes. Do not brown the garlic. Remove the garlic and slowly pour the oil over the peppers. Occasionally run a rubber spatula carefully around the sides of the jar to allow the oil to fill all the air pockets. Refrigerate.

Half an hour before using, take the peppers out of the oil and drain them. Let them come to room temperature and serve them as part of an antipasto or use them in other recipes. *Makes 1 quart (1 liter).*

Dried Tomatoes

Dried tomatoes have an intense flavor and can be used in a multitude of recipes, from vinaigrettes to sauces and soups. They keep for months in a cool, dark, dry place or when frozen. If you have a problem with meal moths, store the tomatoes in the freezer. To soften and rehydrate them for use in sandwiches and sauces, pour boiling water or stock over them and let them sit for a few minutes, or until the skins are soft. The liquid from the rehydrated tomatoes is great for adding flavor to dishes.

Wash the tomatoes and drain them dry. Cut the tomatoes in half (cut 2- to 3-inch [5- to 7.5-cm] paste tomatoes into three or four slices) and place them skin-side down on the dehydrator tray. Put the tray in the food dehydrator and follow the directions for drying tomatoes. Different models have different heat- and time-setting recommendations.

If you have a gas oven with a pilot light, you can put the tomatoes on racks and dry them using only the heat from the pilot light (keep the door closed). It takes about 3 days to dry tomatoes this way.

Tomatoes can also be dried in the sun in hot, arid climates. Lay the tomatoes out on a clean window screen that is plastic-coated (or otherwise not made of metal). Place the screen in a very sunny location and cover it with another screen to keep off the flies. Bring the tomatoes in at night to get them out of the dew. Depending on the weather, they will dry in 3 to 7 days. Dry them until they are leathery and not sticky.

Transfer thoroughly dried tomatoes into zippered, freezer-strength plastic bags. Store them in a cool, dry, dark closet.

Basil in Parmesan

This recipe, from Rose Marie Nichols McGee, of Nichols Garden Nursery in Oregon, is a great way to preserve the taste of basil for the winter. It's been so popular, she's had it in her herb catalog since 1982. As she says,

"I never tire of fresh tomatoes sprinkled with this blend. Use it on salads, pasta, and fresh or cooked tomato dishes. This recipe makes a good basis for a later preparation of pesto. Small jars frozen and presented as gifts later in the year will be much appreciated." It stays fresh in the refrigerator for one week. Freeze it for longer storage.

1 bunch fresh green basil
Approximately ³/₄ cup (65 g) Parmesan cheese, freshly grated

Rinse the basil and dry it in a salad spinner. Roll a handful of basil leaves into a bunch and with a sharp knife cut the leaves into a thin chiffonade. Repeat the process with the rest of the basil. You should have about 1¹/₄ cups (55 g) chopped. In a half-pint canning jar with a tight-fitting lid, layer ¹/₄ inch (6 mm) of Parmesan cheese on the bottom, then layer ¹/₄ inch (6 mm) of basil, then layer another ¹/₄ inch (6 mm) of Parmesan, and so on. Press down firmly on the top to remove any air pockets, and then sprinkle on a final layer of Parmesan. *Makes about 2 cups (75 g).*

PESTO

Pesto is generally defined as a paste of olive oil, garlic, nuts, Parmesan cheese, and fresh basil and is a specialty of the area around Genoa, Italy. It is served as a sauce for pasta or is used as a flavoring for soup. But many modern chefs adhere to a more general definition, making a pesto with cilantro, peanuts, and peanut oil; mint with corn oil and walnuts; or even dry, without oil. The dry pesto has fewer applications, but

All sorts of herbs can be used to make pesto. Rosemary is ideal for making a dry pesto to serve on minestrone soup or over a rich lamb stew.

again, it is a way to preserve that fresh flavor. Pestos are versatile as toppings for pizza, pastas, stews, and soups. Most can be incorporated into sauces for meats and mixed with yogurt, mayonnaise, or sour cream into dressings for salads. Finally, pesto freezes well and is a way to preserve the herb's flavor after the season is past. The following recipes are for a classic basil pesto and a dry rosemary pesto. They may be frozen in small canning jars and kept for four to six months. When freezing, leave out the cheese and add it just before serving. To prevent discoloration, place plastic wrap directly on the surface of the pesto before you freeze it.

Classic Pesto

Serve this pesto over fettuccine, or other pasta, either dry or fresh. Try combining cooked green snap beans with the noodles for a lovely variation.

3 garlic cloves
2 cups (85 g) fresh basil leaves
$^{1}/_{4}$ cup (25 g) pine nuts or walnuts
$^{1}/_{2}$ teaspoon salt
$^{1}/_{4}$ teaspoon freshly ground black pepper
$^{3}/_{4}$ cup (190 ml) extra-virgin olive oil
$^{1}/_{2}$ cup (45 g) freshly grated Parmesan cheese

In a blender or food processor, combine the garlic, basil leaves, nuts, salt, pepper, and half the oil. Purée, slowly adding the remaining oil. Transfer the mixture to a bowl and add the grated cheese, mixing thoroughly. Use immediately or cover with plastic wrap, since basil pesto turns brown if exposed to air. If you are going to serve this pesto over pasta, you may need to add a few tablespoons of cooking water to the pesto to make it the right consistency for the pasta. *Makes approximately 1¼ cups (300 g).*

Rosemary Pesto

Sometimes I make this pesto in a blender, but I find I must mince the garlic and finely chop the rosemary, or they don't blend properly. This pesto is added to a minestrone or tomato soup or sprinkled over a pizza before baking.

3 large garlic cloves, minced
Handful of fresh Italian parsley leaves
Leaves from 2 (3-in/8-cm) sprigs of fresh rosemary
6 tablespoons freshly grated Parmesan cheese
$^{1}/_{2}$ dried hot pepper

In a mortar, put the garlic, parsley, rosemary, Parmesan cheese, and hot pepper. Pound the ingredients with the pestle to a crumbly paste and serve. *Makes about $^{1}/_{2}$ cup (40 g).*

Mexican essentials

The following recipes are some of the building blocks of Mexican cuisine, and can enrich countless dishes. Many Mexican meals require quite a bit of preparation time, but this time commitment can be lessened for individual meals by keeping these standard components on hand.

Refried Beans

Refried beans are a staple in Mexico and one we could all use in our repertoire. I had problems making them until Luis Torres, friend and cooking maven, walked me through the process. He found I'd not been cooking the beans and oil long enough before mashing them. They were too firm to get smooth and velvety.

The thickness of the finished bean purée is a matter of taste. A thicker paste is good for burritos and tacos so they won't drip, but a moist, creamy product is great to accompany huevos rancheros. To change the consistency of your refried beans add more or less bean liquid or water. Some cooks prefer to use more oil than is called for here; others like less.

1 lb (500 g) dry pinto, Peruano, or
   black beans
1 to 3 cloves garlic
6 cups (1.5 liter) boiling water
¹/₂ cup (125 ml) corn oil
¹/₂ to 1 teaspoon freshly ground cumin
Salt and freshly ground black pepper

In a large pot, wash and sort through the beans and eliminate foreign matter and spoiled beans. Add garlic and water; bring back to the boil. Turn the heat to low and simmer beans for 1 to 1¹/₂ hours or until tender. (Freshly har-vested beans take less time than older ones.) Drain the beans and reserve the liquid.

Pour the oil in a large frying pan. Turn the heat on high and carefully (they splatter) add drained beans and 1¹/₄ cups (315 ml) of the bean liquid. Simmer, stirring occasionally, for 6 to 8 minutes or until the beans are fairly soft. Add more liquid if the beans are getting dry. Turn the heat down and mash them a little at a time with a potato masher. Again, add more bean liquid if they get too dry. Add the cumin and salt and pepper, adjust the seasonings, and remove from heat. *Serves 4 as a side dish.*

Toasted Vegetables

The most common vegetables that are toasted in Mexico are onions, garlic, tomatoes, tomatillos, and small green chilies. The handiest and most traditional way to toast them is on a comal. This flat cast-iron griddle is invaluable for Mexican cooking, inexpensive, and available from many mail-order sources and Mexican markets. (I now keep one on the stove at all times for warming tortillas and toasting bread, nuts, vegetables, and herbs.)

To toast vegetables, heat the comal over fairly high heat and place whole tomatoes, hulled tomatillos, halved and quartered large onions, small green chilies, or unpeeled garlic on the comal. Turning occasionally (chef's tongs work especially well), cook for 3 to 5 minutes or until the vegetables start to blacken. Once cooked, sweat tomatoes and chilies for a few minutes in a paper or plastic bag for ease of peeling. Peel the toasted vegetables. They are now ready for making into sauce, soup, or salsa. (Rick Bayless, Mexican cooking maven, recommends lining the comal with aluminum foil before roasting tomatoes to avoid the juicy mess. Diana Kennedy suggests that, if roasting large quantities, you broil the tomatoes on a baking sheet a few inches from a hot broiler for 10 to 12 minutes, turning them occasionally.)

If you don't have a comal, use a dry cast-iron frying pan or griddle. Roasting vegetables on an outdoor charcoal barbecue or gas grill works well too, especially for large batches of vegetables.

Roasted Peppers

Roasting large chilies calls for a different technique, as the peppers are seldom smooth and the skins need to be evenly charred. You can roast a few large peppers by holding them on a fork in a gas cooktop flame for

Left: Beans, primarily dry ones, are a staple in the Mexican diet. The dozens of varieties differ subtly in both flavor and texture, as seen in these two dishes of refried beans made with different types of beans. **Above:** Comals like this one are important tools in the Mexican kitchen. If you don't have one of your own, you can use a dry cast-iron frying pan.

a few minutes. Turn them constantly to make the skin blacken and blister evenly. If you have an electric stove, put them under the broiler and char them the same way, or char them over a gas grill. If using the broiler of a home oven, brushing the chilies with a little oil helps them to roast more quickly and evenly. (The goals are to have the chilies roasted but still somewhat firm inside and to make the skins come off readily.) Put the charred peppers in a paper bag to steam for a few minutes for ease of peeling. Scrape the skin off, and stem and seed the chilies. At this point, you can leave them whole for stuffing, cut them into strips, or chop them, depending on the recipe. (If your hands are sensitive, use latex gloves. To prevent burning your eyes, do not rub them while you work with chilies.) Roasted chilies (and tomatoes, too) freeze well in sealable freezer bags.

Dried Chilies

Mexicans appreciate the deep, toasty flavors of dried chilies and use them in salsas, most soups and stews, and numerous appetizers. Because the flesh of the majority of hot peppers is thin, they are easy to dry. Further, some of the varieties arguably taste better in that form. One thick-walled pepper, the jalapeño, is also dried—in this case, by first smoking it. The smoked and dried jalapeño, called a chipotle, adds a lovely smoky flavor to sauces and soups.

To dry thin-walled peppers, first choose peppers that are fully ripe and unblemished. If you live in an arid climate, you can dry peppers on a screen in a warm dry place out of the sun and dew. Stir the peppers every day or so to promote even drying. If the peppers are large, they dry more readily if you cut a slit in the side. In rainy climates, or if the peppers are unripe, they must be dried in a dehydrator, in a gas oven using only the pilot light, or in an electric oven at 150°F (65°C) for about 12 hours. Cut slits in the side of the peppers and rotate them occasionally. (The tiny bird peppers dry so readily they need only to be placed on a sunny windowsill for a few days.) Once your peppers are brittle, to keep them dry and the insects under control, store them in a jar with a lid or in a sealable freezer-strength plastic bag.

To bring out their rich flavors, dried chilies are often toasted on a hot comal for 30 seconds or until they release their perfume. To reconstitute the chilies, break them into a few pieces, put them in a bowl, pour hot water over them, and let them sit for 20 to 30 minutes before draining. For some recipes the water is retained and added to the recipe. The chilies can then be ground into a paste and added to sauces or combined with garlic and other spices to create a mole or salsa.

MOLES AND SALSAS

No discussion of Mexican cuisine would be complete without covering salsas and Mexico's special sauces.

Salsas are ubiquitous in Mexico and the fastest-growing segment of the North American condiment market as well. Chilies, both fresh or dried, are the common denominator in salsas and the infinite variations range widely in flavor and spiciness, depending on the technique and ingredients used. While the most common salsas are tomato-based, in Mexico, one also enjoys salsas of different roasted, fresh chopped chilies mixed with a little lime juice, green salsas made from either cactus paddles or cucumbers, tomatillo-based salsas, and even one made with ground pumpkin seeds and Mexican crema (similar to crème fraîche).

For centuries, most salsas and moles were made into a paste using a lava rock *molcajete*, a mortar, and a *tejolote*, a pestle. This process grinds the ingredients and produces a characteristic desirable texture. Few cooks today use these ancient tools; the blender makes it easier to purée sauces and some salsas (not a food processor, as it does an uneven job). Ingredients to be blended must first be chopped or they will blend unevenly and become too soupy by the time the large pieces are done. Blend on low to control the texture. Blender

aside, many fresh tomato and tomatillo sauces have the best texture if you chop the ingredients by hand.

Mole Verde (Green Mole with Vegetables and Seeds)

Moles are an integral part of Mexican cuisine and have numerous variations. Nancy Zaslavsky, author of invaluable books on Mexican cooking, including *A Cook's Tour of Mexico* and *Meatless Mexican Home Cooking*, contributed this recipe. It was inspired from her work with Juanita Gomez de Hernández in Tehuacán. Nancy recommends serving it over beans, chunks of steamed green vegetables, or rice dishes. I like it in tamales. (For information on toasting vegetables and roasting large chilies, see page 35.)

6 poblano chilies
1 lb (500 g) tomatillos
4 jalapeños, stemmed, with seeds intact
1 white onion, quartered
4 cloves garlic
2 tablespoons vegetable oil, divided
$^1/_2$ lb (250 g) unsalted, raw shelled green pumpkin seeds (pepitas)
$^1/_4$ cup (25 g) chopped walnuts or pecans
$^1/_4$ cup (35 g) chopped almonds
2 cups (500 ml) vegetable broth or water
2 teaspoons salt
6 grinds of black pepper
$^1/_2$ cup (15 g) chopped flat-leaf parsley

Toast the poblanos. Peel, stem, and remove the seeds and put them in a blender container.

Husk the tomatillos and wash them. Toast the tomatillos and jalapeños on a comal and put them in the blender. Toast the onions and garlic and put them in the blender. Blend the vegetables.

Toast the pumpkin seeds (they will jump around and pop). Put them in the blender. Toast the nuts. Blend them with the pumpkin seeds and $^1/_2$ cup (125 ml) water.

In a large, heavy pot, heat 1 tablespoon of oil. Add the seed-nut paste and fry it, stirring, for 30 seconds. Turn the heat down to simmer and add the tomatillo mixture, adding more oil, if necessary. Add the broth, salt, and pepper. Cook until all the broth is incorporated and the sauce is slightly thickened, about 20 minutes. Blend the parsley with enough water to purée and add. Taste carefully and adjust the seasonings. *Serves 6.*

Salsa Verde (Tomatillo Salsa)

This traditional green salsa is made from tomatillos. Try it with roasted or barbecued pork, scrambled eggs, tamales, burritos, and in tacos. It keeps for about 5 days in the refrigerator. (For more salsa recipes, see pages 127 and 130.)

20 large tomatillos about 1$^1/_2$-in (4-cm) in diameter
1 tablespoon oil
2 or 3 fresh serrano or jalapeño peppers, minced
1 medium white onion, minced
2 cloves garlic, minced
$^1/_4$ teaspoon sugar
Salt to taste
2 tablespoons minced fresh cilantro

Husk the tomatillos and wash them. Put them in a saucepan, add 1/2 cup (125 ml) water, and simmer them, covered, until just tender, about 5 minutes. Drain, cool, and mince.

Heat the oil in a nonstick sauté pan and add the tomatillos, chilies, onions, garlic, and sugar. Cook the vegetables over medium heat, stirring, for about 5 minutes. Add the salt. Cool, stir in the cilantro, and serve. *Makes 2$^1/_2$ cups (625 ml).*

Left: Mexican salsas and moles are spicy affairs. Chilies, of course, but also toasted garlic and onions and many spices, including black pepper, cumin, coriander, cloves, and cinnamon, are common ingredients. **Above:** Although salsa is often made with tomatoes (left), tomatillo salsa (right) is a tasty—and green!—alternative.

Sweet things

With a little imagination, your garden can enrich every meal of the day—and desserts, too! Sweet edible flowers and herbs can be used to add an exciting new dimension to sugar or honey and make delicious flavorings for fancy treats like jelly and flavored whipped creams.

Lavender Sugar

Making fragrant lavender sugar takes about a month. Use it to flavor cookies, lemonade, and hot or cold teas.

½ cup (15 g) dried lavender leaves and flowers
2 cups (450 g) superfine sugar, or finely ground granulated sugar (sometimes called baker's sugar)

In a jar with a tight lid, mix the dried lavender and the superfine sugar. Shake it occasionally to equally distribute the sugar. After about 3 to 4 weeks the oils of the lavender will have flavored the sugar. Sift the mixture through a large strainer to remove the lavender. Store the sugar in its jar for up to a year. *Makes 2 cups (450 g).*

Rose Petal Honey

Robin Sanders and Bruce Naftaly of Le Gourmand restaurant in Seattle use this honey to make baklava, transforming an already delicious dessert into something divine. They also suggest using this honey in other desserts, meat glazes, and tea. When using rose honey in your favorite baklava recipe (*Joy of Cooking* has one; eliminate the orange water, though), also sprinkle a few chopped honeyed rose petals on the nut mixture and use fresh or candied roses as garnish.

Petals from 10 unsprayed roses, preferably the fragrant old-fashioned types, such as 'Belle of Portugal,' any of the rugosa roses, damasks, and the eglantine rose
1 cup (250 ml) honey

Rinse the rose petals briefly in cold water and dry them in a salad spinner.

In a nonaluminum pan, slowly heat the honey until runny. With a wooden spoon stir in the rose petals, cover, and steep over extremely low heat for 45 minutes, stirring occasionally. Remove from heat and let cool for 15 minutes. Strain the honey through a fine sieve, and reserve petals for another use. *Makes about 1 cup (250 ml).*

Quick Rose-scented Geranium Apple Jelly

This is a creation of Carole Saville, author and herb expert. If you want a more strongly flavored jelly, add another scented geranium leaf to the recipe.

¼ cup (30 g) fresh raspberries
3 large rose-scented geranium leaves

One 10-oz (285-g) jar apple jelly
Petals from 18 rose-scented geranium
flowers

Place the raspberries in a strainer placed over a small bowl. With the back of a spoon mash the berries against the side of the strainer to extract the juice. Set the juice aside.

Wash and thoroughly dry the geranium leaves. Finely chop the leaves and tie them in a square of cheesecloth.

Pour the apple jelly into a saucepan and quickly bring it to a boil. Stir in the reserved raspberry juice, then add the bag of geranium leaves. Stir the mixture for 1 minute, then cover tightly, and remove from heat. Let the jelly cool for about 20 minutes. Uncover the pan and, with the back of a spoon, press the bag of geranium leaves against the side of the pan to extract all the juice. Discard the bag of geranium leaves. Stir in the geranium petals. Pour the still-warm jelly into a hot, sterilized jar. Put on the lid and allow the jelly to cool (it should take approximately an hour). Refrigerate and use within two weeks. *Makes 10 ounces (285 g).*

Mint Whipped Cream

Nobody can boast of the health aspects of cream, but it sure does taste good. Add mint to the cream, whip it to serve with chocolate cake, steep it with savory for a sauce for potatoes and leeks, or steep it with basil and add it to custard. Flavored creams are the greatest.

¹/₄ cup (20 g) chopped fresh
spearmint or peppermint
1¹/₂ cups (375 ml) whipping cream
1¹/₂ tablespoons granulated sugar
¹/₄ teaspoon vanilla extract

Place the mint and cream in a small saucepan over a low heat until small bubbles just begin to form around the sides of the pan. Do not let the cream boil. Cool. Pour the cream through a mesh strainer and discard the mint. Chill.

Just before serving, place the cream in a mixing bowl and whip it until the cream just starts to hold its shape. Add the sugar slowly as you mix. Add the vanilla and continue to whip until soft peaks form. *Makes 1¹/₂ cups (180 g).*

Far left: In a pretty jar, rose petal honey can be a wonderful gift. **Left:** Rose-scented geranium jelly can be used between layers of pound cake or piped into delicate rolled cookies to make little treats to serve at a shower or fancy party. **Above:** Decadent and delicious, mint-flavored whipped cream is a good complement to rich, dark chocolate desserts.

Sensational salads

Mesclun

Mesclun is a Provençal term for a mix of many varieties of young red and green lettuces, arugula (rocket), endives, and chervil, either grown together or grown separately and then mixed in the salad bowl. Mesclun is traditionally served with a simple vinaigrette. There are endless variations using different vinegars, lemon juice, sprinklings of fresh herbs, and all different types of croutons and seasonings.

For the dressing:
2 tablespoons red wine vinegar
Salt and pepper
6 to 7 tablespoons extra-virgin
   olive oil

For the salad:
4 to 6 large handfuls of mixed
   mesclun greens

To make the dressing: Mix the vinegar, salt, and pepper and using a whisk blend in the oil to taste.

To make the salad: Toss the dressing gently with the mesclun greens and serve. *Serves 4 to 6.*

Basic garden salad

One of the great things about a salad is that you can usually take whatever is in the garden, produce section, or farmers' market and mix it in the bowl, from early spring to late fall—even in the winter if you have a cold frame or a little greenhouse. Most times the base of your salad will be a lettuce or some other neutral green. To determine quantities, figure on one large handful of greens per person. To the greens you can add all sorts of goodies like baby beet thinnings, wild chickweed, pea shoots, cooked vegetables, meats, nuts, and croutons. The list is almost endless. The following is a jumping-off-type recipe; the point is to let your imagination dictate what goes into your glorious salads.

For the dressing:
1¹/₂ tablespoons balsamic or rice
   wine vinegar
1 garlic clove, minced
1 teaspoon Dijon-style mustard
3 to 4 tablespoons extra-virgin
   olive oil
1 teaspoon fresh dill or basil
Salt and freshly ground black pepper

For the salad:
1 small head butter lettuce
1 small head Oak Leaf lettuce
1 small Belgian endive, base
   removed and leaves separated
1 small head of frisée
10 arugula (rocket) leaves
6 dill flowers
1 large red chard stem, cut into 2-in
   (5-cm) pieces

To make the dressing: In a small bowl, mix the vinegar, garlic, mustard, oil, and herbs; add salt and pepper to taste; and whisk until emulsified.

To make the salad: Combine the greens in a large bowl. Pour the dressing over the greens, and toss. Garnish with dill flowers and chopped chard stem. *Serves 4.*

Wild party salad

This salad has a festive feeling and a bright minty flavor. It can include a dozen varieties of greens, even wild ones like violets or miner's lettuce, or a tamer mix of three or four lovely lettuces and baby spinach. Much depends on what's available in your garden or at the market.

For the dressing:
- 5 tablespoons avocado oil
- 5 tablespoons chardonnay
- 3 tablespoons white wine vinegar
- 1/4 teaspoon salt
- 1/4 teaspoon freshly ground black pepper
- 2 teaspoons finely chopped fresh mint

For the salad:
- 1 large head romaine lettuce
- 2 large heads leaf lettuce
- 1 large handful arugula (rocket), stems discarded
- 1 small bunch of young spinach
- 2 to 4 handfuls of greens, such as baby bok choy or chard, upland cress or watercress, violet leaves, miner's lettuce, minutina, and chrysanthemum leaves, or other seasonal greens
- 1/2 cup (20 g) violet and violas, petals of calendula and chive blossoms, small florets of mustard or broccoli blossom
- Garnish: whole calendula or viola flowers, florets of mustard or broccoli, and a few sprigs of whole greens

To make the dressing: In a small mixing bowl, combine the oil, wine, vinegar, salt and pepper, and mint. Stir the ingredients with a wire whisk. Refrigerate until ready to serve.

To make the salad: Wash the greens and dry them in a salad spinner or on paper towels. Tear the greens into bite-size pieces and place them in a very large serving bowl. Cover the bowl with plastic wrap and refrigerate until ready to serve.

Wash the edible flowers and put the stems in a glass of water or place the flowers between damp paper towels. Refrigerate until ready to serve.

To serve, remove the petals from the calendula and chive flower heads, break the mustard or broccoli flower heads into small florets, and set them aside. Stir the dressing, drizzle it over the greens, and toss lightly to coat the greens. Sprinkle the chive and calendula petals, mustard and broccoli florets, and whole viola or violet flowers over the salad. Garnish one side of the bowl with a cluster of whole calendula or viola flowers, mustard or broccoli florets, and a few whole greens. *Serves 6 to 8.*

Watermelon spicy salad

This salad is a blend of traditional Thai flavors. The following recipe was inspired by a TV show I saw featuring chefs Mary Sue Milliken and Susan Feniger. I missed writing down their recipe, so I tried to re-create it. Here is my re-creation.

For the dressing:
- 1/4 cup (65 ml) fresh lime juice
- 1/4 cup (65 ml) white grape juice
- 1 tablespoon nam pla (Thai fish sauce)
- 1 tablespoon chopped mint or cilantro
- 1 or 2 jalapeño peppers, minced
- Garnish: mint or cilantro

For the salad:
- 1 small head Bibb lettuce
- 4 cups (600 g) watermelon cubes, seeded if necessary
- 16 to 20 small American shrimp, cooked
- 1/2 cup (65 g) chopped roasted salted peanuts

To make the salad: Line 4 individual salad plates with the Bibb lettuce leaves. Put 1 cup (150 g) of the watermelon cubes on each plate. Add the shrimp, and sprinkle the peanuts over the salad. In a small bowl, whisk together the dressing ingredients and distribute evenly over each plate. Garnish with sprigs of fresh mint or cilantro. *Serves 4.*

Flower confetti salad

Chartreuse butter lettuces and the warm colors of flower petals can dress up an everyday salad or start off a festive meal. A salad can be especially dramatic when prepared at the table. Pick flowers as close to serving time as possible. Put the stems in a glass of water and refrigerate.

For the dressing:

2 tablespoons rice wine or champagne vinegar

Salt and freshly ground black pepper

1 teaspoon frozen white grape juice or apple juice concentrate

3 or 4 tablespoons extra-virgin olive oil

For the salad:

1 large or 2 small heads of Bibb lettuce

1 large handful of mixed baby greens

6 to 8 organically grown edible flowers such as nasturtiums, calendulas, violas, pansies, rose petals, or borage flowers

To make the dressing: In a small bowl, combine the vinegar, salt, pepper, and juice concentrate. Whisk in the oil until blended.

To make the salad: Wash the lettuce and baby greens and dry them in a salad spinner or gently pat them dry with paper towels. In a large salad bowl, break the lettuce leaves into bite-size pieces and add baby greens. If not serving immediately, cover the bowl lightly with plastic wrap and refrigerate.

Wash the flowers gently, lightly pat them dry with paper towels, and gently pull off the petals. In a small bowl, stir the petals to mix the colors and make a confetti. You should have about 1/3 cup (15 g) of loosely packed petals.

Stir the dressing, pour 3 or 4 tablespoons over the lettuce and greens, and toss. Add more dressing if needed, but be careful not to overwhelm the salad. Divide the salad equally among four salad plates. Scatter a small handful of flower-petal confetti over each individual salad and serve. *Serves 4.*

Garden bouquet salad with lemon-herb vinaigrette

Here's an elegant and exotic salad from Renee Shepherd of Renee's Garden.

For the dressing:

1 small scallion (green onion), chopped fine

1 teaspoon Dijon-style mustard

2 or 3 tablespoons lemon juice

1 tablespoon dry white wine

1 egg yolk

1 tablespoon minced fresh parsley

1 tablespoon minced chive flower petals or chopped fresh chives

1/4 teaspoon salt

Pinch of freshly ground black pepper

3/4 cup (190 ml) olive oil

For the salad:

2 small heads radicchio (or red-leaf lettuce as a second choice)

2 handfuls mâche (corn salad)

2 small heads Bibb lettuce

12 to 14 leaves (2 handfuls) young arugula (rocket) or watercress

2 or 3 fresh sorrel leaves

3/4 cup (30 g) fresh green and purple basil leaves

1/2 cup (20 g) calendula petals

1/4 cup (10 g) borage flowers

To make the dressing: With a whisk, combine all the ingredients except the oil. Slowly whisk in the oil, beating continually until the mixture is thoroughly blended. Season to taste. Refrigerate until ready to use.

To make the salad: Wash and dry the greens. Reserve 6 to 8 leaves of radicchio or red lettuce. Tear the remaining radicchio, mâche, Bibb lettuce, arugula, and sorrel into bite-size pieces and combine them with the basil leaves in the center of the salad bowl. Line the outer edges of the bowl with the reserved radicchio or red lettuce. Sprinkle the calendula petals and borage flowers around the outside border.

Stir the dressing again and pour it over the salad after presenting it at the table. *Serves 6.*

Riot of color salad

How about a really colorful salad for a special occasion? Use your imagination and the prettiest edible flowers from your garden.

For the dressing:

1¹/₂ tablespoons white wine vinegar
3 to 4 tablespoons sunflower oil
1 tablespoon clover or wildflower honey
Salt and freshly ground black pepper

For the salad:

1 large head romaine lettuce
1 head butter lettuce
1 small head frisée
4 to 6 young leaves of yellow chard
About a dozen organically grown edible flowers such as yellow and blue violas, purple pansies, nasturtiums, yellow calendulas, and red dianthus

To make the dressing: In a small bowl, combine the vinegar, sunflower oil, honey, salt and pepper. Set aside.

To make the salad: Arrange the romaine lettuce, butter lettuce, and chard leaves on a large colorful platter. Separate the flowers into petals, reserving some whole. Sprinkle the greens with flower petals and garnish with the whole blossoms. Bring the salad to the table and let diners dress their own salad. *Serves 4.*

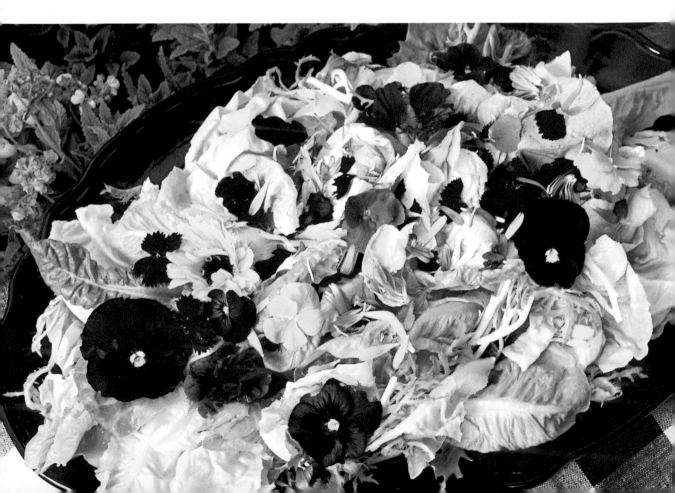

Tangelo and kiwifruit salad with orange blossoms

This citrus salad is lovely to look at, and the flavors are both familiar yet slightly different. Taste your citrus petals before adding them to the dressing. Expect some bitterness, but if they are very harsh try blossoms from another tree. The point of adding a few citrus blossoms to the dressing is to infuse the tangelo juice with a lovely aroma and to deepen the citrus flavor.

6 medium tangelos, divided, or 3 tangelos and 1 cup (250 ml) of bottled fresh tangerine juice
1 tablespoon fresh lemon juice
5 lemon, tangerine, or orange blossoms, divided
1 tablespoon honey (optional)
2 kiwifruit

To make the salad: Squeeze 3 of the tangelos and put the juice (or the bottled tangerine juice) in a medium bowl. Add the lemon juice and the petals of 3 of the orange blossoms. If the tangelos are not very sweet, add a tablespoon of honey. Peel and section the remaining 3 tangelos, peel and slice the kiwifruit, add them to the juice mixture, and stir to cover the fruit. Refrigerate for a few hours.

To serve: Divide the fruit among four serving dishes. Pour the tangelo juice over the fruit and garnish with the remaining citrus blossom petals. *Serves 4.*

Rainbow slaw

This slaw is fairly low in calories for a party dish, and it's packed with nutrition. Serve it with grilled meats or as part of a buffet.

For the dressing:
Juice of 1 lemon
$^2/_3$ cup (170 ml) white wine vinegar
1 teaspoon salt
$^3/_4$ teaspoon celery seeds
$^1/_3$ cup (85 ml) vegetable oil
3 or 4 tablespoons frozen apple juice concentrate
Freshly ground black pepper

For the salad:
8 cups (800 g) finely sliced green cabbage (1 large head)
1 cup (35 g) thinly sliced chard leaves
2 cups (300 g) finely sliced carrots
1 small sweet onion, thinly sliced
1 cup (50 g) thinly sliced red chard stems

To make the dressing: In a small bowl, mix together the lemon juice, vinegar, salt, celery seeds, oil, apple juice concentrate, and pepper (to taste) and stir until the ingredients are fairly well blended.

To make the salad: Place the cabbage in the bottom of a large salad bowl. Creating a decorative pattern, arrange the chard leaves, then the carrots, then the onions, and finally the chard stems.

Pour the dressing over the slaw and serve. The salad may be refrigerated for a few hours, but the dressing separates, and the red chard stems lose some of their color if the salad sits too long. *Serves 8 to 10.*

Oriana's cabbage salad

This recipe could also be called Latin Coleslaw; it was given to me by my young neighbor, Oriana Mendy. She says it tastes best when made using tomatoes from a friendly neighbor.

$^1/_2$ medium green cabbage, finely shredded
3 or 4 ripe tomatoes, diced
1 large ripe avocado, cut into $^1/_2$-in (13-mm) cubes
3 or 4 scallions (green onions), finely sliced
$^1/_4$ to $^1/_3$ cup (5–10 g) chopped fresh cilantro
Juice of 1 lime
Salt

Place the cabbage, tomatoes, avocado, and scallions in a large bowl. Sprinkle the cilantro, lime juice, and salt (to taste) over the cabbage mixture and gently stir to combine the ingredients. Serve immediately in a large bowl or prepare individual serving plates. *Serves 4.*

Romano bean salad with grilled tuna

This mid-summer treat is great with crusty bread, and just right for a light fancy lunch.

For the dressing:
1/2 cup (125 ml) extra-virgin olive oil
3 to 4 tablespoons fresh lemon juice
Salt and freshly ground black pepper

For the salad:
1/2 small red onion, thinly sliced
1 teaspoon salt
1 medium red bell pepper
1 1/2 lbs (725 g) green and gold Romano beans, sliced 1 in (2.5 cm) on the bias (about 4 cups)
Optional: 3-in (8-cm) sprig of fresh winter savory
8 to 10 leaves butter or leaf lettuce
1/2 to 2/3 lb (250–340 g) fresh yellow-fin tuna fillet

To make the dressing: In a small bowl, whisk the olive oil, lemon juice, salt, and pepper together until they emulsify. Set aside.

To make the salad: Put the onion slices into a small bowl, cover them with cold water, and add the salt. Mix together and let them sit for 1 hour to remove some of the bite.

Meanwhile, roast the pepper over the flame of a gas stove, or under a broiler until charred. Place the charred pepper into a brown paper bag and let it cool. When it is cool enough to handle, remove the seeds, scrape off the skin, and cut the pepper into 1/2-inch (13-mm) strips. Set them aside.

Steam the beans with the (optional) savory over simmering water about 5 minutes or until just tender. Drain the beans, discarding the savory. Shock the beans in ice water until they are chilled and drain again. Drain the onion slices. Arrange the butter lettuce leaves on a serving platter or in a large flat bowl. Arrange the beans, onion slices, and peppers over top.

Meanwhile, preheat the grill. Brush the tuna with 1 tablespoon of the dressing mixture. Over high heat, grill the tuna to medium rare for about 7 minutes on each side. Cut the fish on the bias into 1/2-inch (13-mm) thick slices and arrange them on the vegetables. Drizzle the remaining dressing over the tuna and the vegetables. Serve immediately. *Serves 4.*

Spicy and sour squid salad

Chef Areeawn Fasudhani, of the Khan Toke Thai House in San Francisco, created this lovely dish. Note that *nam pla*, listed among the ingredients, is a salty fish sauce commonly used in Thai cooking. It is bottled like soy sauce and is available in Asian markets.

1/2 lb (250 g) cleaned and sliced squid (about 1 cup)
1 tablespoon finely chopped lemongrass
2 tablespoons lime juice
1 1/2 tablespoons nam pla (Thai fish sauce)
1 tablespoon sliced shallots
1 teaspoon chili powder, or finely chopped hot peppers to taste

1 teaspoon finely chopped coriander root (if available)
1 teaspoon chopped scallion (green onion)
1 teaspoon cilantro
Lettuce or cabbage leaves
10 mint leaves
Sprigs of fresh cilantro

Dip the squid into boiling water for 30 seconds; drain, then put it in a bowl. Season with the lemongrass, lime juice, nam pla, shallots, chili powder, coriander root, scallions, and cilantro. Toss lightly. Place the mixture on a serving plate next to lettuce or cabbage; decorate with the mint and cilantro leaves. Serve immediately. Eat by scooping up squid and juices together with the lettuce or cabbage leaves. *Serves 2 as salad or 4 as appetizer.*

Jody's sprout salad

Jody is my garden manager and a longtime sprout enthusiast. This is her wonderful salad.

For the dressing:

¹/₈ teaspoon salt

1 garlic clove, peeled and chopped

¹/₄ cup (65 ml) extra-virgin olive oil

2 tablespoons balsamic vinegar

¹/₄ teaspoon Dijon-style mustard

Freshly ground black pepper to taste

For the salad:

1 medium head leaf lettuce

1 small bunch spinach

1 small bunch baby red chard with stems, or ¹/₂ lb (250 g) mixed baby greens

1 cup (100 g) assorted sprouts: radish, mung, sunflower, alfalfa, or other sprouts, rinsed and drained

¹/₂ cup (40 g) slivered almonds, chopped

Garnish: nasturtium flowers and leaves

To make the dressing: In a small bowl, pour the salt over the chopped garlic and crush it with a fork to make a paste. Add the oil, vinegar, mustard, and pepper. Whisk the ingredients together until the mixture is creamy.

To make the salad: Wash and spin-dry the lettuce, spinach, and chard. Tear the leaves into bite-size pieces and place them in a large salad bowl. Sprinkle the sprouts on top. Dress and toss the salad. Garnish with nasturtium flowers and leaves. *Serves 6 to 8.*

Spinach and watercress salad with savory mayonnaise

Robin Sanders and Bruce Naftaly at Le Gourmand restaurant in Seattle contributed this cool autumn and early spring recipe. You can add cold, moist poached chicken to this salad—it goes very well with the sage in the dressing. If you prefer a lighter flavor, substitute safflower, peanut, or corn oil for half the olive oil. In winter, use dried calendula petals as a garnish. All the ingredients except the greens must be around 70°F (20°C).

For the dressing:

2 egg yolks

3 tablespoons balsamic vinegar, divided

¹/₂ teaspoon salt

¹/₄ teaspoon freshly ground white pepper

1 teaspoon chopped fresh sage (optional)

1 cup (250 ml) kalamata (or other virgin) olive oil

¹/₃ cup (85 ml) glace de viande (dark-brown reduced brown stock)

For the salad:

A generous amount of spinach and watercress leaves for each serving in a 2:1 ratio (or substitute young nasturtium or arugula [rocket] leaves for the watercress)

Garnish: calendula petals

To make the dressing: In a large bowl, use an electric beater on medium-high speed or a whisk to beat the egg yolks well. Add 1 tablespoon of the vinegar, and the salt, pepper, and sage (if desired). While beating, very slowly add the oil and the remaining vinegar by droplets until half the oil is used; add the rest in a slow stream. Beat in the glace de viande. Transfer the dressing to a storage or serving container using a rubber spatula. Refrigerate if you will not be using it immediately.

To make the salad: Warm the dressing to room temperature by beating it in a bowl before tossing it with the greens. Dress the greens to taste and garnish with calendula petals. You may have more dressing than you need; refrigerate the remainder. *Serves 8 or more.*

Radicchio and mâche with figs and hazelnuts

This salad is rich and filling, with a nice balance of bitter and sweet. For a party presentation, line the bowl with the radicchio, layer the mâche on top, and sprinkle on nuts and figs. Dress the salad at the table and toss.

For the dressing:
1/4 cup (65 ml) hazelnut or extra-
  virgin olive oil
3 tablespoons balsamic vinegar
Salt and freshly ground black pepper

For the salad:
1 small head radicchio
3 cups (120 g) mâche (corn salad)
5 dried figs, divided
¹/₄ cup (2 oz/60 g) hazelnuts
1 tablespoon baking soda

To make the dressing: In a small bowl, whisk together the oil, vinegar, salt, and pepper.

To make the salad: Tear the radicchio into bite-size pieces. In a large salad bowl, mix it with the mâche. Coarsely chop two of the figs and add them to the salad; halve the remaining three figs and set them aside.

To peel the hazelnuts, bring 2 cups (500 ml) of water to a boil in a large sauce-pan. Add the baking soda. Boil the hazelnuts for 5 minutes. Preheat the oven to 350°F (175°C). Drain and rinse the nuts, and rub off the skins with your fingers. Place the hazelnuts on a cookie sheet and roast them for 10 minutes, or until they're a light brown. Cool the hazelnuts, chop them coarsely, and add them to the salad.

Pour the dressing over the salad and toss lightly. Garnish with the fig halves and serve. *Serves 4 to 6.*

Endive salad with oranges and pistachios

This salad is lovely on a buffet table or served as part of a light luncheon.

For the dressing:

1 tablespoon extra-virgin olive oil
1 tablespoon white wine vinegar
2 tablespoons freshly squeezed orange juice
¹/₄ teaspoon salt
¹/₄ teaspoon freshly ground black pepper

For the salad:

2 Belgian endives
1 cup (30 g) young spinach leaves
2 oranges
1 cup (90 g) red seedless grapes
¹/₄ cup (35 g) shelled pistachios, coarsely chopped

To make the dressing: Combine the oil, vinegar, orange juice, salt, and pepper.

To make the salad: Pull apart the endive leaves. Wash and spin-dry them. Arrange the leaves in a concentric circle on a serving plate. Intersperse the spinach leaves. Peel the oranges and cut them into slices. Arrange the oranges on the endive and spinach leaves. Add the grapes and sprinkle on the pistachios. Drizzle dressing over the greens and grapes. *Serves 4.*

Hearty greens with pears, blue cheese, and chives

Serve this salad as a first course or increase the quantities by 50 percent and use it as the centerpiece of a luncheon menu.

For the dressing:
¹/₄ cup (65 g) nonfat yogurt
¹/₃ cup (45 g) crumbled blue cheese
1 teaspoon Dijon-style mustard
¹/₂ teaspoon Worcestershire sauce
2 teaspoons white wine vinegar
¹/₄ teaspoon curry powder
3 tablespoons snipped chives
1 teaspoon honey
Salt and freshly ground black pepper

For the salad:
4 large handfuls of mixed salad greens: lettuces, spinach, mâche (corn salad), endive, and radicchio
1 tablespoon lemon juice

2 ripe, medium Comice or Bartlett pears
8 thin triangular slices of blue cheese
Garnish: chive leaves and blossoms

To make the dressing: In a small bowl, stir gently the yogurt, blue cheese, mustard, Worcestershire sauce, vinegar, curry powder, chives, and honey to combine. Add salt and pepper to taste. Adjust the seasoning if necessary. Refrigerate until ready to serve.

To make the salad: Wash and dry the greens in a salad spinner or on paper towels. Just before serving, set out four large salad plates. Put a handful of greens on each plate. Into a small bowl, pour the lemon juice and 4 tablespoons water. Cut each pear into ¹/₃- to ¹/₂-inch (8–13-mm) thick slices and dip the slices into the lemon water to prevent them from browning. Arrange four to six slices of pear on top of the greens on each plate. Place two slices of blue cheese on the side of each plate. Garnish with chive leaves and blossoms. Pour the dressing in a serving bowl. Serve immediately. *Serves 4.*

Tangy salad with roasted garlic dressing

This salad appeals to mustard and garlic lovers alike. The greens are primarily members of the tangy mustard family, and the richness of the roasted garlic rounds out the flavors and gives body to the dressing.

For the dressing:

4 roasted garlic cloves (see right), peeled

1 raw garlic clove, minced

1 teaspoon mustard powder

4 tablespoons extra-virgin olive oil

3 tablespoons red wine vinegar

Dash of salt and freshly ground black pepper

For the salad:

1 small head romaine lettuce

1 small head frisée

1 small bunch watercress

1 small handful tatsoi leaves

1 small handful red mustard leaves

Garnish: mustard or nasturtium flowers

To roast the garlic: Preheat the oven to 350°F (175°C). Place 1 whole head of garlic on a baking pan and roast it for 20 or 30 minutes, or until it's soft. Cool the garlic. The pulp can now be squeezed out to use in the dressing. (Extra roasted garlic can be served as a spread for rustic bread.)

To make the dressing: Into a small mixing bowl, squeeze the roasted garlic pulp. Add the raw garlic and mustard powder and work them into a smooth paste with a spoon. Gradually stir in the olive oil and vinegar. Add salt and pepper to taste. Beat the mixture with a wire whisk until the ingredients emulsify.

To make the salad: Wash and dry the greens in a salad spinner or on paper towels. Tear the leaves into bite-size pieces and arrange them in a large salad bowl. Before serving, stir the dressing again, pour it over the greens, and toss. Garnish with the mustard or nasturtium flowers. *Serves 4.*

Garden celebration salad

This dish is a busy assembly project and takes lots of bowls, but it requires little in the way of technique. It provides plenty of room for creativity and makes a spectacular party salad. Some of the vegetables work best when cooked, others when raw. As with any good garden recipe, the ingredient list is fluid and can be varied by the season and by what's in the garden or market.

The salad has 5 layers of colors, each layer with a slightly different flavor combination. Suggested vegetables and herbs for the orange/gold layer include slivered carrots, chopped orange peppers, gold beets, and sliced gold tomatoes; for the yellow layer: yellow zucchini, wax beans, chopped yellow peppers, and sliced yellow tomatoes. For the green layer choose among: chopped lettuces, cabbages, baby spinach, snow pea pods, scallions, and any of the herbs: parsley, chives, basil, fennel, or savory. For the red layer I suggest: red beets, tomatoes, and peppers; and for the purple layer: chopped red cabbage, magenta radicchio, and blue potatoes.

I've given directions for stacking the prepared vegetables in a glass trifle bowl to reveal the colors through the sides of the bowl, but the same ingredients can be laid out on a large colorful platter instead. If you use a clear glass bowl, the moisture from the vegetables will condense on the bowl when you add hot ingredients or when you bring it out of the refrigerator. Let the bowl stand at room temperature before serving time to give the condensation time to evaporate.

For the garlic vinaigrette:

2 garlic cloves, minced

1 tablespoon Dijon mustard

1/2 cup (125 ml) extra-virgin olive oil

1/4 cup (65 ml) white wine vinegar

Freshly ground black pepper and salt

For the honey vinaigrette:

1/4 cup (65 ml) extra-virgin olive oil

1 teaspoon honey

2 tablespoons white wine vinegar

1/8 teaspoon red pepper flakes

For the salad:

1 lb (500 g) yellow zucchini, sliced

1 lb (500 g) yellow wax beans cut in 2-in (5-cm) sections

1 medium yellow sweet pepper, chopped

1 lb (500 g) green zucchini, sliced

1 lb (500 g) green beans cut in 2-in (5-cm) sections

4 tablespoons chopped scallion (green onion) greens

1/2 teaspoon minced fresh savory

1 small red cabbage, shredded

1 medium red sweet pepper, chopped

3 red paste tomatoes, sliced

1/3 teaspoon red pepper flakes

1 medium orange sweet pepper, chopped

3 orange paste tomatoes, sliced

3 medium golden beets, steamed 30 minutes, peeled and sliced

To make the vinaigrettes: In two separate bowls, whisk together the ingredients for each of the vinaigrettes and set them aside.

To prepare the salad layers: Bring a large pot of salted water to a boil. First cook the yellow zucchini, then the yellow wax beans for 3 minutes each, or until just tender. After each batch is done, remove the vegetables from the cooking water with a slotted spoon and refresh them for a couple of seconds in a bowl of ice water to keep their color. Drain the vegetables and put them in a small bowl. Add the yellow pepper and toss with 1/4 cup (65 ml) of garlic vinaigrette.

Repeat the process with the green zucchini and green beans. When the vegetables are at room temperature, toss the contents of the bowl with 1/4 cup (65 ml) more of garlic vinaigrette. Set aside to marinate for about 10 minutes, then sprinkle with the scallions and savory.

Mix the shredded red cabbage with the remaining garlic vinaigrette and set it aside.

In a fourth bowl, combine the red pepper, red tomato, and red pepper flakes.

In a fifth bowl combine the orange peppers, the orange tomatoes, and the golden beets.

To assemble the salad: You will need a glass bowl 5 inches (15 cm) wide and 8 inches (20 cm) deep. A traditional footed trifle bowl works well. Each layer of vegetables needs to be about 1 inch (2.5 cm) thick.

Build the salad by first layering the marinated yellow vegetables 1 inch (2.5 cm) deep on the bottom. On top of this create a green layer. Create the third, purple layer with the red cabbage.

Cover with the red layer and finally the orange layer. Glaze the top of the salad with the honey dressing. Serve immediately. *Serves 12 to 14 for a buffet.*

Henry's salad with vietnamese coriander

Henry Tran is both a friend and landscaping contractor with whom I work. He has helped me identify a number of Vietnamese greens and herbs over the years and generously shared the traditional ways they are used in Vietnam. The following is one of his salad suggestions.

For the dressing:
2 tablespoons rice vinegar
2 teaspoons low-sodium soy sauce
1 teaspoon finely chopped fresh Vietnamese coriander (rau ram)
$^1/_2$ teaspoon finely chopped mint or spearmint
$^1/_8$ teaspoon hot red pepper flakes
Pinch of salt
$^1/_8$ teaspoon finely chopped fresh ginger root (optional)

For the salad:
2 teaspoons sugar
1 small Vidalia, Maui, or other sweet white onion, sliced paper thin
6 cups (450 g) butter lettuce, washed and dried
Garnish: 4 sprigs fresh Vietnamese coriander

To make the dressing: In a small mixing bowl, combine the rice vinegar, soy sauce, Vietnamese coriander, mint, chili flakes, salt, and the ginger, if being used.

To make the salad: Pour 1$^1/_2$ cups (375 ml) of water into a medium bowl. Add the sugar and stir until it has dissolved. Separate the onions into rings and add them to the bowl. Allow the mixture to sit for 30 minutes.

In a large bowl, toss the lettuce with the dressing, coating the leaves well. Divide the lettuce among four plates. Drain the onions. Divide and place them atop each serving. Garnish each salad with a sprig of Vietnamese coriander. *Serves 4.*

Fennel salad with red peppers

This is a basic fennel salad to which I have added the bright colors of red peppers and their wonderful depth of flavor.

For the dressing:

2 tablespoons lemon juice
2 tablespoons extra-virgin olive oil
2 tablespoons chicken stock
1 tablespoon honey
Salt and freshly ground black pepper to taste

For the salad:

2 medium fennel bulbs, trimmed (1¹/₂–2 lbs/725 g–1 kg)
2 red bell peppers, thinly sliced
Garnish: fennel leaves

To make the dressing: In a small bowl, combine the lemon juice, olive oil, chicken stock, honey, salt, and pepper and whisk them thoroughly. Set aside.

To make the salad: Wash and, if necessary, remove the tough stringy outer layer of the fennel bulbs. Set aside a few of the light green inner leaves for garnish. Very thinly slice the fennel on a mandolin or using a sharp knife. (You should have about 1 quart/1 liter of wafer-thin slices.) To prevent discoloring, immediately dress the fennel and mix well. Allow to marinate by refrigerating for at least 2 hours before serving.

To serve, drain the fennel slightly, reserving the extra liquid. Place the fennel on a large serving plate, arrange the sliced peppers over the fennel, drizzle with the reserved dressing, and garnish with the fennel leaves. *Serves 3 to 4.*

Duck breast salad

This is truly an elegant salad and perfect for an intimate dinner party. It is best served as a first course and then followed by a seafood entrée.

The duck is succulent and tender if cooked to medium rare and begins to get drier and tougher as it approaches thoroughly done.

1 teaspoon black peppercorns
2 boneless duck breasts (1 lb/500 g total), skin and fat removed
$1/4$ teaspoon salt
1 tablespoon vegetable oil

For the greens:
1 small heart of romaine
3 cups (90 g) lightly packed spinach
2 cups (75 g) lightly packed mâche (corn salad)
1 small head frisée

For the dressing:
1 shallot, minced
1 tablespoon dry sherry
1 tablespoon red currant jelly
2 tablespoons extra-virgin olive oil
2 tablespoons balsamic or sherry vinegar
$1/4$ teaspoon fresh thyme

Preheat the oven to 450°F (235°C).

On a flat surface, break up the peppercorns into a coarse grind by rubbing them with the bottom rim of a small cast-iron frying pan. Rub the broken peppercorns into the sides of both duck breasts and season the meat with salt. Heat the vegetable oil to quite hot in a heavy cast-iron frying pan. Add the duck and cook one side for about $2^1/2$ minutes, or until brown. Turn the breast over and place the frying pan in the oven. Roast the duck for 6 to 8 minutes, or until medium rare.

While the duck is cooking, arrange the greens on a large platter, cover, and refrigerate.

Remove the duck from the frying pan and place on a cutting board to rest. Put the frying pan over medium heat, add the shallots, and sauté until they're soft, about 3 minutes. Deglaze the pan with 2 tablespoons water and the sherry. Add the red currant jelly and simmer until the jelly has melted. Transfer the sauce into a bowl, add the olive oil, vinegar, and thyme. Whisk until blended.

Remove the platter of greens from the refrigerator. Slice the duck breast on a diagonal into thin slices. Slide a long spatula under one of the sliced breasts and fan the slices out over the arranged greens. Repeat the process with the other breast. Drizzle the still-warm dressing over the duck and some of the greens. Serve immediately. *Serves 4.*

Caesar salad

Tijuana, Mexico, was the unlikely birthplace of this famous salad. It remains one of the best treatments for crisp, fresh romaine. Worcestershire sauce, not anchovies, was part of the original recipe. They are both listed here as optional; use one or the other.

For the dressing:
5 or 6 tablespoons extra-virgin olive oil
1 garlic clove, pressed
4 tablespoons fresh lemon juice
1 teaspoon Worcestershire sauce (optional)
Dash of Tabasco sauce
4 to 6 anchovy filets, diced and mashed (optional)

For the salad:
1 large head romaine lettuce
1 egg, boiled 1 minute
$1/2$ teaspoon salt
Freshly ground black pepper
$1/2$ cup (50 g) freshly grated Parmesan cheese
Garlic croutons

To make the dressing: In a large salad bowl, combine the olive oil, garlic, lemon juice, Worcestershire sauce, and Tabasco. Add the anchovy filets, if you're using them, and blend them well into the dressing.

To make the salad: Add the romaine to the dressing and toss. Crack the egg into the salad; sprinkle the salad with salt, pepper, and Parmesan cheese; and toss again until all the leaves are well coated. Add the croutons and toss one final time. *Serves 6.*

Cool white salad

This recipe was created especially for me by Carole Saville, who designs culinary gardens for restaurants and writes herb books. While not traditional, it captures the spirit of Mexico.

For the dressing:
2 tablespoons lime juice
$^1/_4$ teaspoon cumin
Salt to taste
Freshly ground white pepper to taste
Pinch cayenne pepper
6 tablespoons corn oil
1 tablespoon cilantro, chopped fine

For the salad:
1 large or 2 small jícamas
Garnish: slices of sweet white onion;
sliced orange halves

To make the dressing: In a mixing bowl, combine lime juice, cumin, salt, white pepper, and cayenne pepper. Slowly whisk in the oil until the dressing is emulsified. Add cilantro and mix again.

To make the salad: Peel the jícama and cut it into thin matchsticks. Pour dressing over jícama and mix well. Garnish with onions and orange. Chill salad in the refrigerator. *Serves 6.*

Note: Jícama, a native of tropical America, is a crispy, sweet root vegetable commonly eaten raw.

Tomato and basil salad

This recipe is a regular summer feature on the menu of John Downey's restaurant in Santa Barbara when local farmers bring John luscious ripe tomatoes and fragrant basil.

For the dressing:
2 tablespoons extra-virgin olive oil
4 tablespoons red wine vinegar
1 garlic clove, minced
¹/₂ cup (20 g) coarsely chopped fresh basil
Salt and freshly ground black pepper
Garnish: green peppercorns (optional)

For the salad:
4 large ripe garden tomatoes, sliced
1 small sweet red onion, thinly sliced

To make the dressing: Combine the oil, vinegar, garlic, basil, and salt and pepper in a small bowl.

To make the salad: Place the tomatoes in a shallow pan. Pour the dressing over the tomatoes and let them sit for about 30 minutes, then remove them with a slotted spoon. Arrange the tomatoes on four serving plates. Divide the onion slices among the plates, garnish with peppercorns, and serve. *Serves 4.*

Salade niçoise

This classic salad is from the south of France; olives and anchovies betray the Mediterranean influence. The beauty of the dish is in its arrangement, which can be done on a serving platter or individual plates.

For the dressing:

4¹/₂ tablespoons red wine (or balsamic) vinegar

2 teaspoons salt, plus extra

Freshly ground black pepper

2 small garlic cloves, finely minced

10 to 12 tablespoons extra-virgin olive oil

2 tablespoons finely chopped fresh tarragon

For the salad:

3 to 5 medium potatoes

1 lb (500 g/3 cups) fresh snap beans, trimmed

20 to 24 peeled baby boiling onions or a jar of pickled onions

1 head butter lettuce, washed, dried, and chilled

3 ripe tomatoes, quartered

1 cup (225 g) quality canned or grilled yellowfin tuna, chilled

3 hard-boiled eggs, halved

¹/₂ cup (70 g) Mediterranean-style olives

Garnish: Tarragon or other fresh herbs and approximately 6 canned anchovy filets

To make the dressing: In a small bowl mix the vinegar, salt and pepper, and garlic. Whisk in the oil. Add the tarragon and stir. Refrigerate.

To make the salad: Boil the whole potatoes until just tender. Drain and rinse them in cold water and slip off the skins. While they're still warm, cut them into ¹/₈-inch (3-mm) slices and in a bowl gently toss with about ¹/₃ cup (85 ml) of the vinaigrette. Set aside.

Bring a large pot of water to a boil. Add a little salt and the beans and boil them until just tender-crisp, about 3 to 5 minutes. Using a slotted spoon, remove the beans from the water, run cold water over them to stop the cooking, and drain.

Add the baby onions to the boiling water and blanch them until they're tender, about 7 minutes. Drain them.

In a small bowl toss the blanched beans and onions (if they aren't pickled) with enough dressing to coat. Just before serving, toss the lettuce leaves with dressing to coat and arrange them on a platter or plates. Arrange the potatoes, beans, onions, tomatoes, tuna, eggs, and olives in distinct clusters on the lettuce, drizzling on the remaining vinaigrette and garnishing with fresh herbs and the anchovy filets. Serve with French bread. *Serves 6.*

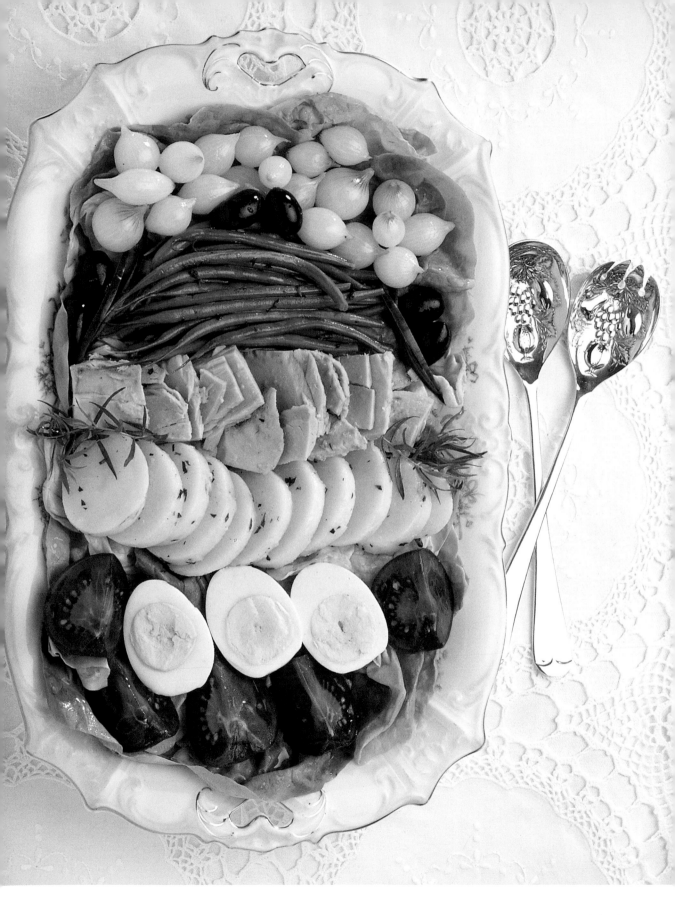

Crab and asparagus salad with fancy greens and sorrel dressing

This is a show-off dish fit for the fanciest "do." Fresh, fresh crab; fresh, fresh asparagus; and fresh, fresh greens all deserve this special pastry presentation.

For the puff pastry shell:
6 tablespoons butter
1 teaspoon salt
1 cup (100 g) flour
4 eggs

For the dressing:
1 cup (250 ml) mayonnaise
1/4 cup (65 ml) yogurt
1 tablespoon Dijon-style mustard
1 garlic clove, minced or pressed
1 tablespoon grated onion
3/4 cup (30 g) sorrel, finely chopped
1/2 teaspoon salt
Freshly ground pepper

For the salad:
1 lb (500 g) asparagus
1 medium head romaine lettuce
1 lb (500 g) Alaska king crab meat
   (about 3 cups)
1/2 lb (250 g) mixed young greens
   such as mâche (corn salad), baby
   butter lettuce or spinach, and tatsoi

To make the pastry: Preheat the oven to 400°F (205°C).

In a 2-quart (2-liter) saucepan, bring 1 cup (250 ml) water to a boil over high heat. Add the butter and salt. As soon as the butter has melted, take the pan off the heat and add the flour all at once. Using a wooden spoon, stir the mixture quickly until the flour is completely blended. Put the pan back over medium-high heat and beat the dough until it comes away from the sides of the pan and forms a loose ball. Remove the pan from the heat. Let it cool for 5 minutes. Stir in the eggs, one at a time, beating thoroughly after each addition. The dough will appear to break apart with each egg but will reform with vigorous stirring. The eggs should be completely incorporated and the dough smooth and glossy.

Spoon the dough into a buttered 9-inch (23-cm) springform pan and spread it evenly over the bottom and up the sides a few inches. Bake for 40 minutes. Turn off the oven. Prick the pastry with a wooden pick in at least a dozen places and leave it in the oven to dry for 10 minutes. Remove the pan from the oven and let it cool completely. Remove the sides of the pan. (This pastry shell may be made up to a day ahead.) Wrap the pastry loosely in aluminum foil and store it in a warm, dry place. Before using, crisp it in a 400°F (205°C) oven for 5 minutes.

To make the dressing: Blend all the dressing ingredients in a small bowl. If the dressing is too thick, thin it with a tablespoon or so of cream or milk.

To make the salad: Wash the asparagus and cut the spears into 2-inch (5-cm) pieces on a diagonal. Cook the asparagus in boiling water for 4 minutes. Drain and set aside.

Wash, dry, and separate romaine lettuce leaves. Set aside six of the tender inside leaves and coarsely chop the rest. You should have about 2 cups (150 g), chopped.

Combine the asparagus, crabmeat, and chopped romaine lettuce in a bowl. Mix with 1 cup (250 ml) of the dressing and refrigerate for up to 1 hour. Just before serving, place the pastry shell on a very large platter and fill it with the crab mixture. Surround the pastry shell with the remaining romaine leaves and the assorted young greens. Pour the remaining dressing in a small pitcher to be used on the greens. *Serves 6.*

Irresistible soups and starters

Cream of roasted pimiento soup

The velvety green cream drizzled on this rosy-red soup makes this perfect for an elegant first course.

1 tablespoon canola oil

1 medium yellow onion, chopped

2 garlic cloves, minced

1 large green poblano or 'Anaheim'
  pepper, roasted, peeled, and
  seeded

10 pimiento or other red bell peppers
  (about 2$^1/_2$ lbs/1.2 kg), roasted,
  peeled, and seeded

2 cups (500 ml) chicken stock or one
  14-oz (500-ml) can of chicken stock

$^1/_4$ teaspoon ground cumin

$^1/_4$ teaspoon salt or to taste

$^3/_4$ cup (190 ml) heavy cream

Pour the oil into a medium nonstick frying pan, heat, and add the onions and garlic. Sauté over medium heat until the onions are translucent, about 7 minutes, and reserve.

In a blender, put the poblano pepper and 1 tablespoon of the chicken stock, and purée to a smooth paste. Using a rubber spatula, scrape the paste into a small bowl, add 1 teaspoon of heavy cream, and stir to combine. (If any lumps remain, force the mixture through a fine sieve.) Pour the green pepper mixture into a plastic squeeze bottle or a small bowl and set aside.

Wash the blender, then place the pimiento peppers, the onion mixture, the remaining chicken stock, the cumin, and salt in the blender and purée. (You may have to do this in two batches.) Pour the pimiento mixture into a saucepan and bring it to a simmer. Remove from the heat and stir in the rest of the heavy cream. Reheat the soup if necessary, but do not allow it to boil or it may separate.

To serve, pour the soup into 4 soup bowls, dividing it equally. Using the squeeze bottle, make a pattern of poblano cream on the soup (or drizzle cream from a spoon in a decorative pattern) and serve immediately. *Serves 4 to 6.*

French onion soup gratinée

Few recipes feature the onion as well as this traditional French onion soup. Carefully browning the onions is the secret to a rich flavor.

4 tablespoons (¹/₂ stick) butter

8 to 10 medium onions (8–10 cups/ 800 g–1 kg), thinly sliced

2 garlic cloves, divided

1 teaspoon sugar

3 tablespoons all-purpose flour

8 cups (2 liters) beef or chicken stock

³/₄ cup (190 ml) dry white vermouth

Salt and freshly ground black pepper

3 tablespoons cognac or brandy

8 slices toasted French bread

2 cups (220 g) grated Swiss cheese, divided

1 tablespoon extra-virgin olive oil

To make the soup: In a large saucepan, melt the butter and stir in the onions and 1 clove minced garlic, cover, and cook them slowly over low heat for about 15 minutes, stirring occasionally. Uncover, stir in the sugar, and cook on low to medium heat for 30 minutes, or until onions are well browned. Stir them often, scraping the bottom of the pan to prevent burning. Sprinkle on the flour and stir for 2 to 3 minutes. Remove pan from heat, slowly stir in the stock and vermouth, and salt and pepper to taste. Cover and simmer on low heat for 30 minutes. Stir in the cognac or brandy. The soup may be either served as is or frozen at this point.

To make the gratin: Preheat the oven to 350°F (160°C). Rub the remaining garlic clove over the toasted bread. Place a little soup in each of eight ovenproof ramekins or soup bowls. Divide ¹/₂ cup (55 g) of the grated cheese evenly among the bowls. Put 1 slice of bread in each bowl; cover with more soup and the remaining cheese. Drizzle oil over each bowl and place in the oven for 20 minutes; then set the bowls under the broiler to lightly brown the cheese. Serve immediately. *Serves 8.*

Lavender-tinted vichyssoise

Vichyssoise is an elegant but easily made first course. Make it with blue potatoes and you'll really delight your guests. To get the lavender effect you need to use the very deep purple varieties. Medium or light blue potatoes will give you a sickly gray, not lavender, soup. Serve this lavender vichyssoise in white or clear glass bowls so the color is featured, garnished with chives and chive florets.

2 tablespoons butter
3 onions, diced (about 3 cups/450 g)
3 to 4 deep-blue potatoes, peeled
    and cubed (about 3 cups/525 g)
1 tablespoon fresh lemon juice
1 cup (250 ml) half-and-half
Salt and freshly ground black pepper
Dash of nutmeg
Garnish: fresh chive leaves and
    flowers

In a large saucepan, melt the butter and sauté the onions over medium heat until softened but not browned, about 7 minutes. Add the potatoes and 3 cups (750 ml) of water. Cover and simmer until the potatoes are tender, 15 to 20 minutes.

Add the lemon juice, half-and-half, and seasonings and purée the soup in a food processor or blender. Chill and serve cold. Garnish by sprinkling the soup with the chives and the chive flowers, separated into florets. *Serves 4.*

Golden gazpacho

This classic Spanish recipe is usually made with red tomatoes and green peppers, but here I put a spin on the ball and make it with gold tomatoes and yellow bell peppers.

7 to 10 medium ripe gold tomatoes
1 large yellow pepper
1 small onion, or 2 to 3 scallions
    (green onions)
2 garlic cloves, minced
$^1/_2$ green Anaheim chili pepper
1 small hot red chili pepper, or to
    taste
1 large or 2 small cucumbers, peeled
1 tablespoon extra-virgin olive oil
$^1/_3$ cup (85 ml) white wine vinegar
$^1/_2$ cup (125 ml) dry white wine
Salt and freshly ground black pepper
3 or 4 sprigs fresh cilantro
Garnish: cilantro sprigs, a slice of
    tomato, or diced avocado

Immerse the tomatoes in boiling water for 30 seconds, or until the skins have loosened. Peel them and remove the seeds and cores. Remove the seeds and membranes from the yellow pepper. Chop the rest of the vegetables coarsely for processing in the food processor or blender (if you use a food processor the soup will have some crunch; using the blender will give a smoother texture).

Process all ingredients in batches, pouring them into a large nonreactive bowl to mix. Refrigerate the soup at least 3 hours before serving. If the gazpacho is too thick, thin it with a little cold vegetable or chicken stock before serving. Taste and adjust seasonings. Serve the soup in individual bowls and garnish each serving as desired. *Serves 4.*

Wonton dumpling soup with oriental chives

Created by Helen Chang, this version of the classic soup is light and savory. The dumpling dough can be purchased already prepared in your supermarket or an Asian market. Spinach can be substituted for the pac choi greens.

For the dumplings:
- 1/3 lb (170 g) ground pork
- 3/4 cup (75 g) finely chopped cabbage
- 1/3 cup (20 g) finely grated carrots
- 1/2 cup (30 g) finely chopped fresh Oriental chive leaves
- 4 tablespoons finely grated peeled fresh ginger root, divided
- 2 tablespoons chopped cilantro
- 1/2 teaspoon freshly ground black pepper
- 1 teaspoon salt
- 1 teaspoon sugar
- 3 teaspoons cornstarch
- 1 egg, lightly beaten
- One 12-oz (340-g) package square wonton skins, thawed if frozen

For the soup:
- 2 quarts (2 liters) chicken broth
- 10 to 12 mushrooms, thinly sliced
- 1 large head of pac choi, green leafy sections cut in narrow strips; large white stems reserved for another use
- Hot pepper sauce (optional)
- 3 teaspoons chopped cilantro leaves

To make the dumplings: In a medium bowl, place the pork, cabbage, carrots, chives, 2 tablespoons grated ginger, cilantro, pepper, salt, sugar, and cornstarch. Add the egg and stir to combine the ingredients.

Place the wonton skins, a few at a time, on a clean work surface. (Meanwhile, keep the rest of the wontons in the package, or place a slightly damp towel over them to prevent them from drying out.) Mound a teaspoon of filling in the middle of each wonton square and then fold to form a triangle or semicircle. Press the edges together to seal, then bend corners toward each other as you would for wontons. (Refer to the wonton package for folding directions.) Place the folded dumplings on a cookie sheet, leaving space between each one. Cover and refriger-ate dumplings when filled, if not using immediately.

When ready to serve bring a large pot of water to a boil and add the dumplings and simmer for 5 to 6 minutes, or until they become translucent. Remove them from the water with a slotted spoon and divide them among 6 bowls.

To make the soup: In the meantime, pour the chicken broth into a large soup pot. Add the remaining 2 tablespoons of ginger. Bring to a simmer and add the mushrooms. Simmer over low to medium heat for one minute. Add the pac choi leaves and chives to the simmering broth. Add hot sauce to taste, if using.

To serve: Fill the bowls with broth and pac choi. Garnish each bowl with chopped cilantro. *Serves 6.*

Potage de rouge vif d'etampes

Rouge Vif d'Etampes is a French heirloom pumpkin reminiscent of Cinderella's coach. In the 1800s Parisian chefs favored it as a base for vegetable stocks. I find it lends itself well to the following rich chowder, served in the French style—in the pumpkin. Serve this dish as you would a hearty chowder or stew.

6 cups (210 g) 1-in (2.5-cm) cubes of homemade-style white bread

1 (10–12-in/25–30-cm) Rouge Vif d'Etampes pumpkin

3 tablespoons extra-virgin olive oil

1 lb (500 g) leeks (about 5 medium), white and pale green parts only, finely chopped (about 5 cups)

1 medium fennel bulb, chopped (about 1¹/₂ cups/130 g)

6 garlic cloves, minced

1 teaspoon powdered saffron

1¹/₂ teaspoons dried thyme

1 tablespoon chopped fresh tarragon

1 teaspoon salt

¹/₂ teaspoon freshly ground black pepper

¹/₄ teaspoon ground red pepper

Approximately 6 cups (1.5 liters) vegetable or chicken broth

Approximately 1¹/₂ cups (375 ml) half-and-half

¹/₂ lb (250 g) Gruyère cheese in ¹/₂-in (13-mm) cubes (about 1¹/₂ to 2 cups)

Preheat the oven to 350°F (175°C).

Put the bread cubes on a cookie sheet and bake them for 10 minutes, stirring once. Remove from oven and set aside.

Cut a 6-inch (15-cm) diameter lid from the top of the pumpkin. With a sharp metal spoon, scrape out the seeds and stringy membrane. Place the pumpkin on a shallow baking pan. If the pumpkin does not sit level on the pan, support the tilting side with a piece of rolled-up aluminum foil.

In a large sauté pan heat the oil and sauté the leeks, fennel, and garlic until tender, about 10 minutes. Turn off the heat and add the saffron, thyme, tarragon, salt, pepper, ground red pepper, and the bread cubes, tossing to mix thoroughly. Pour in the chicken broth and half-and-half, stir gently and ladle the mixture into the pumpkin. The pumpkin should be filled within 2 inches (5 cm) of the top. Distribute the cheese cubes on top and replace the lid.

Bake the pumpkin for about 1¹/₂ hours and then remove the lid and bake for another ¹/₂ hour, or until the pumpkin flesh is tender and the cheese is golden brown. If the skin starts to pucker around the outside, test for doneness. Watch carefully as the pumpkin will fall apart if overcooked.

Transfer the pumpkin to a large, warm serving platter or bowl. To serve, use a large serving spoon to scoop out some of the soup into each bowl, then scrape some of the flesh from the pumpkin and add it to the soup. Be careful not to break through the skin, as the liquid will leak out. *Serves 4.*

Miso soup

Miso soup is a traditional Japanese soup, eaten most often at breakfast. Miso paste is made from fermented soybeans and can be found in Asian and natural food stores in plastic tubs. There are all different kinds of miso—ranging in color from blonde to rich reddish-brown—depending on the ingredients from which it is made, the length of the fermentation process, and season. Miso contains acidophilus—the "helpful" bacteria found in yogurt—which will perish if miso is boiled.

Some versions of this soup are made with dashi (bonito flake stock) and kombu (seaweed). The version that appears here is suited more to Western tastes and is a great way to get acquainted with this lovely soup. After you have made it a few times try adding some kombu and/or dashi to the simmering water—but be careful, as the flavor from these ingredients can overpower your soup. Put the dashi in cheesecloth and use it as a "teabag" to flavor your miso gently. Kombu contains agents that accelerate the softening of the soup's vegetables while they cook. If used, both the dashi and the kombu should be removed from the soup just before the water begins to boil.

1-in (2.5-cm) piece of fresh ginger
   root, sliced
1 medium carrot, minced
4 oz (125 g) firm tofu, in ¹/₂-in
   (13-mm) cubes
4 tablespoons miso paste (more or
   less to taste)
2 scallions (green onions), white
   part only, thinly sliced

Bring 1 quart (1 liter) of water and the ginger slices to a boil. Simmer for 5 minutes, then remove the ginger. Add the minced carrot and tofu, and simmer for another 2 minutes. Take the soup off the stove and allow to cool for 1 to 2 minutes. Add the miso and stir gently until it dissolves. Scatter the minced scallion on top and serve immediately. *Serves 4.*

Thai chicken soup with pigeon peas

This lovely light soup is a great beginning to a Thai meal or Chinese stir-fry. Some folks enjoy the fish sauce that gives an authentic Thai taste; others prefer to leave it out.

2 tablespoons vegetable oil

1 frying chicken (3–3$^1/_2$ lbs/1.5–1.7 kg), cut in 6 or 7 pieces

1 large onion, chopped

3 ribs celery, chopped

2 medium carrots, chopped

3 stalks lemongrass, chopped in 2-in (5-cm) pieces and slightly crushed to release flavors

1$^1/_2$ tablespoons grated fresh ginger root

4 garlic cloves, minced

4 Kaffir lime leaves

3 whole dried chilies

$^1/_2$ teaspoon ground coriander seeds

Salt and freshly ground black pepper

2 cups (300 g) shelled fresh pigeon peas or green peas (preferably fresh)

2 small scallions (green onions) sliced thinly, including 1 in (2.5 cm) of the greens

$^1/_3$ cup (20 g) chopped fresh cilantro

1 tablespoon lime juice

Optional: 1 tablespoon Thai fish sauce

In a very large sauté pan, heat the oil on medium. Add a few chicken pieces and brown on all sides. Repeat the process with the remaining chicken. Transfer the browned chicken to a large soup pot. Pour off the excess fat from the pan and add the onions. Sauté until translucent, about 7 minutes. Add the onions to the chicken along with 2 quarts (2 liters) of water. Add the celery, carrots, lemongrass, ginger, garlic, lime leaves, chilies, and ground coriander and bring to a boil. Skim off and discard any foam, reduce the heat, then simmer for 45 minutes.

Pour the chicken and liquid through a colander. Pour the stock back into the soup pan and let the fat rise to the top. Skim off and discard most of the fat on the surface. Meanwhile, cool and separate the chicken meat from the bones and skin, and add the meat back to the stock. You should have about 3 cups (375 g) of chicken meat.

Bring the soup back to a boil and add the pigeon peas and scallions and cook for about 5 minutes, just until the peas are tender. Add the cilantro, the lime juice, and the (optional) fish sauce to taste.

Leek and potato soup with sorrel

This heart-healthy soup is thick and satisfying. It possesses all the richness of leeks but is balanced by the tangy sorrel. Serve it on a cold winter evening in front of the fire with a fine cheese and crusty bread.

1 tablespoon butter
2 tablespoons vegetable oil
2 medium onions, finely chopped (about 1 cup/150 g)
7 large leeks with most of the green removed, coarsely chopped (approximately 4 cups/360 g)
5 medium Yukon Gold or other boiling potatoes (approximately 1¹/₂ lbs/680 g), peeled and grated

Approximately 8 cups (2 liters) of homemade or low-sodium chicken broth
1 cup (40 g) chopped fresh sorrel leaves
1 teaspoon chopped fresh tarragon
Salt and freshly ground black pepper

In a large soup pot, melt the butter and add the oil and onions; over medium heat sauté them for about 5 minutes, or until soft. Add the leeks and sauté 5 more minutes. Add the potatoes and chicken broth and simmer until tender, about 20 minutes. Add more chicken broth if the soup is too thick. Add the sorrel and tarragon, and salt and pepper to taste. Adjust seasonings if necessary. Serve hot. *Serves 4.*

Summer squash and corn chowder

This soup uses copious amounts of summer squash and is substantial enough to eat as a light supper. Serve it with corn bread and a green salad.

To remove kernels from the cob, cut a small piece off the blunt end to make it straight across, place the cob blunt-end down on a cutting board, and use a sharp knife to cut off the kernels. (Mail-order companies carry a gizmo for cutting the kernels off more easily.)

7 or 8 young 5- to 6-in-long (13–15-cm-long) summer squash (about 2 lbs/1 kg)
2 tablespoons unsalted butter or vegetable oil
1 large onion, finely chopped
¹/₂ teaspoon dried thyme
2 cups (350 g) fresh sweet corn kernels (about 5 ears of corn)
2¹/₂ cups (625 ml) milk
1 cup (250 ml) heavy cream
Salt and freshly ground black pepper to taste
¹/₈ to ¹/₄ teaspoon ground red pepper
Garnish: sour cream

If you can pierce the skins easily with your fingernail, the squash do not need peeling; otherwise, peel them. Grate the squash; you should have about 8 cups (900 g). Steam the squash in a large steamer until tender, approximately 15 minutes. Mash the squash and set it aside.

In a large Dutch oven, melt the butter and over medium heat sauté the onion and thyme for about 5 minutes until translucent but not brown. Remove from heat and add the squash, corn, milk, and cream. Season with salt and peppers. Over medium heat stir the mixture to heat it thoroughly; do not bring the mixture to a boil, or it will curdle. Serve garnished with sour cream. *Serves 4 to 6.*

Tortilla soup

This rich and surprising soup is one of my favorite dishes. Its many flavors contrasting with the crisp tortillas and creamy avocados give your mouth a lot to think about. Serve it as a first course as is, or add beans and chicken meat for a filling entrée. As with many Mexican dishes, the garnishes are integral and allow diners to season the dish as they please. See page 35 for more information on toasting vegetables. (See photo on pages 72–73.)

For the broth:
4 cloves garlic, unpeeled
1 white onion, peeled
6 large paste tomatoes
8 cups (2 liters) chicken stock
2 tablespoons lard or vegetable oil
1 teaspoon dried oregano
Salt and freshly ground black pepper
   to taste

For the garnish:
2 chipotle peppers
2 dried ancho peppers
2 cups (500 ml) vegetable oil, divided
6 to 8 stale corn tortillas
1 large ripe avocado
$^1/_2$ lb (250 g) queso fresco, or mozzarella or Monterey Jack
$^1/_4$ cup (65 ml) plus 1 tablespoon
   crema or sour cream
$^1/_2$ cup (25 g) chopped cilantro
3 limes, quartered

To make the broth: Heat a dry comal or cast-iron frying pan until very hot. Toast the garlic cloves in their skins until golden. Cut the onion into 8 sections and toast them in the same manner. Toast the tomatoes until their skins blister. Peel and seed the tomatoes. Peel the garlic. In a blender, purée the toasted garlic, onions, tomatoes and $^1/_4$ cup (65 ml) of the chicken stock. This can be done in two batches.

In a large soup pot, heat the lard. Carefully, because it splatters, add the purée. Reduce the heat and cook, stirring, about 10 to 15 minutes until the purée gets thick and darkens in color. Pour in the remaining chicken stock and the oregano; simmer for about 20 minutes. Season with salt and pepper to taste.

To make the garnish: Remove the stems and seeds from the chilies and cut them into strips $^1/_8$ inch (3 mm) wide. In a frying pan, heat 1 tablespoon of the vegetable oil and fry the chilies, stirring, for 30 seconds. Drain them on a paper towel and set them aside. Stack the corn tortillas; cut them into quarters and then into strips $^1/_4$ inch (6 mm) wide. Add the remaining oil to the frying pan; heat the oil and fry the tortilla strips until they are golden. Remove them from the oil with a slotted spoon and drain them on a paper towel; set aside. Cut the avocado and the queso fresco into 1-inch (2.5-cm) cubes.

To serve the soup: Reheat the broth and ladle individual servings into 4 shallow bowls. Add a few avocado and cheese cubes, sprinkle with fried chilies, and top with tortilla strips. Add a tablespoon of crema, sprinkle with cilantro, and serve with lime wedges. Pass separate bowls of the garnishes so diners can add more if they want to fine-tune their dish. *Serves 4.*

Note: The three most important cheeses used in Mexican cooking are queso fresca, a soft, mild melting cheese—if not available, substitute with mozzarella or Monterey Jack; queso anejo (including cotija), an aged, crumbly, strong-flavored cheese—substitute with a mild feta; and the creamy, rich crema Mexicana that is similar to crème fraîche and sour cream.

Spring vegetable soup with parsley dumplings

This is a basic soup that can be varied from season to season and from garden to garden. Serve with a rustic bread and a salad on the side.

For the stock:

1 chicken, approximately 4 lbs (2 kg)
1 onion, unpeeled
4 celery ribs
2 large carrots
2 garlic cloves
1 bay leaf
2 teaspoons thyme
2 teaspoons salt

For the soup:

2 cups (350 g) halved or quartered baby potatoes
1½ cups (230 g) sliced carrots (about 4 medium carrots)
1 cup (225 g) sliced celery (about 2 ribs)
1½ cups (225 g) shelled young peas (about 1 lb/500 g unshelled)
1½ cups (about 1 lb/500 g) sliced asparagus (1-in/2.5-cm pieces)
1 cup (100 g) sliced scallions (green onions)
2 cups (150 g) young spinach leaves
2 cups (150 g) young dandelion greens
Salt and freshly ground black pepper

For the dumplings:

1 egg
½ cup (60 g) all-purpose flour
3 tablespoons parsley, minced
½ teaspoon salt
⅛ teaspoon freshly ground nutmeg

To make the stock: Remove the skin and fat from the chicken. Cut it into pieces and set aside the breasts. Put the legs, thighs, wings, back, and neck into a large stockpot. Add the onion, celery, carrots, garlic, bay leaf, and thyme. Add 5 quarts (5 liters) of cold water and the salt and bring to a boil. Cover the stockpot and simmer over low heat for 2 hours. Remove the chicken and vegetables from the pot. Discard the vegetables, reserve the chicken, and set aside the broth.

To make the soup: Bring the stock to a boil and add the reserved chicken breasts, the potatoes, carrots, celery, and peas. Simmer for 10 minutes, then add the asparagus and scallions and simmer for 5 more minutes. Remove from heat. Remove the chicken breasts and drain them.

To make the dumplings: In a small bowl, blend the egg, flour, parsley, salt, and nutmeg with a fork until smooth. Bring the soup to a rolling boil. Dip a soup spoon into the boiling liquid, then use it to scoop out a small amount of batter from the bowl. Drop the spoonful of batter into the soup. The batter will drop easily from the spoon if you first dip the spoon into the boiling liquid each time. The dumplings rise to the surface when they are done. Cut the chicken breasts into cubes; remove the meat from the reserved thighs, wings, and back; and add them to the soup. Add the spinach leaves and dandelion greens and adjust seasoning with salt and pepper. Heat the soup to serving temperature and ladle it into warm bowls. *Serves 6.*

Fancy carrot and onion soup

This is a world-class soup! The sweet, bright flavors of carrots contrast beautifully with the dusky flavors of the lovage, coriander, and parsley in the onion soup garnish. The presentation is most dramatic if you serve the soup in individual shallow bowls.

4 cups (600 g) sliced carrots
2 tablespoons vegetable oil
2 cups (300 g) chopped onion
1 garlic clove, finely chopped
1 1/2 cups (375 ml) chicken broth
2/3 cup (170 ml) half-and-half, divided
1 tablespoon coriander or cumin seeds
2 stalks fresh lovage or fresh Italian
   parsley
Garnish: small sprigs of dill or lovage,
   or carrot leaves

To make the carrot soup: Steam the carrots until tender. In a large pan, heat the oil and sauté the onions until translucent, add the garlic, and sauté 1 more minute. In a food processor or blender, purée the onion mixture. Transfer 1/2 cup (120 ml) of the onion purée to a small saucepan and set it aside. Leave the remaining onion mixture in the food processor.

Add the steamed carrots to the food processor and blend until smooth. Transfer the mixture to a saucepan, add the chicken broth, stir, and simmer 1 minute. Remove the carrot soup from the heat and set it aside.

To make the onion soup: In a dry, heavy frying pan, lightly toast the coriander or cumin seeds—keep stirring to prevent them from burning. In a saucepan, heat 1/3 cup (85 ml) of the half-and-half, add the toasted coriander or cumin seeds and the lovage or Italian parsley. Remove from the heat, and let the mixture steep for about 30 minutes to blend the flavors. Strain the seeds and herbs and discard them. Pour the flavored half-and-half into the saucepan with the reserved onion purée.

Before serving, reheat the carrot soup and stir in the remaining 1/3 cup (85 ml) of the half-and-half, bringing it almost to a boil. Reheat the onion mixture. In both cases, do not let the mixtures boil or they will curdle.

To serve, half fill four individual shallow soup bowls with carrot soup. In the middle of each soup bowl, carefully ladle about 1/4 cup (65 ml) of the onion mixture.

Garnish with small carrot leaves, a sprig of lovage, or dill. *Serves 4.*

Citrus dip for begonia blossoms

The slightly crisp texture and sweet citrus flavor of begonias can be a spectacular ice-breaking appetizer. The blossoms come in many splashy colors, and a platterful makes a lovely centerpiece for a buffet table.

1 tablespoon honey
1 tablespoon frozen orange juice
   concentrate
1 teaspoon orange zest
1/2 teaspoon lemon zest
1/2 cup (125 g) nonfat yogurt
4 large organically grown tuberous
   begonia flowers

In a small bowl, combine the honey, orange juice concentrate, and orange and lemon zests. Add the yogurt and mix well. Pour the yogurt mixture into a small, decorative bowl, cover it with plastic wrap, and refrigerate until ready to serve.

Just before serving, gently wash the begonia blossoms and remove each of the petals at its base. Place the bowl of flavored yogurt on a large platter and arrange the petals in a decorative pattern around the bowl. Serve the appetizer within the hour to prevent the petals from wilting. *Serves 4 to 6.*

Melon and prosciutto appetizer

When I visited Italy years ago, we tried an appetizer of melon slices with prosciutto at dinner one night and were instant fans of this classic dish. A piece of prosciutto was lightly wrapped around each piece of melon and eaten out of hand. The sweet perfume of the melon in contrast to the salty rich taste of the prosciutto was not to be forgotten. Once home, I made this recipe and it was such a hit with all my guests I often have it when melons are at their peak.

In the fall, wanting to extend the season of this wonderful dish, I tried making it with crisp, fresh 'Fuyu' persimmons and it, too, was fabulous! It is now an easy fall classic for Thanksgiving. Instead of a cantaloupe I substitute 4 large or 6 medium 'Fuyu' persimmons that are crisp but fully ripe.

1 ripe cantaloupe
12 paper-thin slices of prosciutto
  (about ¹/₃ lb/170 g)

Slice the melon in half and remove the seeds. Cut it in quarters and remove the rind. Slice the quarters in thin slices and arrange them on a serving plate. Cut the prosciutto slices in 2- to 3-inch (5–8-cm) pieces and arrange on the plate among the melon slices. Cover with plastic wrap and refrigerate if not serving for a few hours. An hour before serving, take platter out of refrigerator and allow fruit and prosciutto to come to room temperature. Remove plastic wrap and serve. *Serves 4 to 6.*

Edible flower canapés

Edible flowers provide a striking palette with which to decorate food. With a small garden of edible flowers you can make your canapés look like edible art.

¹/₂ cup (25 g) snipped fresh dill or chive leaves

1 lb (500 g) natural cream cheese, softened

2 large loaves of dense sandwich or rustic-style unsliced bread, or 2 packages melba toast

A selection of edible flowers, 4 or 5 dozens: nasturtiums, borage, calendulas, pineapple sage, runner bean flowers, pansies, violas, violets, and mustard flowers

Herb leaves: sage, parsley, mint, dill, and basil

In a mixing bowl, add the dill and 3 tablespoons of water to the cream cheese and mix until smooth. If the mixture is too thick, add a little more water.

Trim the crusts off the bread and cut it into slices ¹/₃ inch (8 mm) thick. Cut the slices into large squares or rectangles 2¹/₂ to 3¹/₂ inches (6–8.5 cm) wide. Spread the cream cheese mixture on the bread—approximately 1 tablespoon per square—and arrange the squares on cookie sheets. Cover them lightly with plastic wrap and refrigerate until ready to decorate.

Carefully wash the flowers and herbs and gently pat them dry on paper towels. Lay them out on damp paper towels and cover with plastic wrap. Refrigerate until ready to use, but not for more than a few hours.

Decorate each canapé square with an edible flower or two and an herb leaf or two. Re-cover the canapés lightly with plastic wrap and refrigerate until serving time. The canapés may be made a few hours in advance, but do not prepare them any earlier, or the garnishes will wilt.

Put a paper doily on a decorative tray, place decorated squares on the tray, and serve. *Serves 6 to 8 as an appetizer.*

Bell pepper ribbon cheesecake

This is a spectacular, unusual first course and is also perfectly suited for a buffet. Serve the cheesecake with slices of avocado and have plenty of chopped cilantro available for garnishing.

For the crust:

2 cups (9-oz/225-g bag) ground restaurant-style white corn tortilla chips

1/2 cup (80 g) pine nuts

1 tablespoon chili powder

4 tablespoons (1/2 stick) unsalted butter, melted

For the filling:

1/4 teaspoon coriander seeds

1 lb (500 g) natural cream cheese, at room temperature

1/4 cup (65 ml) heavy cream

1 teaspoon cumin seeds, roasted and ground

2 eggs, at room temperature

4 large red bell peppers

1/2 teaspoon salt

1 1/2 teaspoons chipotle powder

Garnish: red pepper slices and fresh cilantro

To make the crust: In a food processor, process the corn chips and pine nuts until they have the consistency of crumbs. Add the chili powder and the melted butter and process for a couple of seconds more. Press the mixture into the bottom and up the sides of a 9-inch (23-cm) diameter removable-bottom springform pan. Refrigerate the crust while you prepare the filling.

To make the filling: Heat a small dry frying pan on the stove, then add the cumin seeds and roast, shaking occasionally until the aromas are released. Cool and then grind.

Put the cream cheese into the bowl of a mixer equipped with the flat beater. Add the heavy cream, cumin, and coriander, and beat on medium speed until the ingredients are well combined. Scrape down the sides of the bowl, add the eggs, and beat for about 1 minute or until light and fluffy. To ensure a smooth filling, scrape down the sides once more and beat 1 minute longer.

Roast the peppers according to the instructions on page 35. Remove the skin and seeds and chop the peppers finely. Reserve a few strips for garnish. In a bowl, blend the chopped peppers with the salt and the chipotle powder.

To make the cheesecake: Preheat the oven to 300°F (150°C). Remove the prepared crust from the refrigerator. Spread one-half of the cream cheese mixture over the crust. Spoon the red pepper mixture on top of the cream cheese. Spoon the remaining cream cheese mixture over the peppers, then smooth over.

You will need to bake the cheesecake in a water bath using a baking dish or roasting pan wider but not deeper than the cheesecake pan. Using heavy-duty aluminum foil, wrap the bottom and sides of the springform pan to prevent water from soaking into the cake. Set the wrapped pan into the baking dish. Bring a kettle of water to a boil.

Set the baking dish with the cheesecake on the lower oven rack and carefully pour the boiling water into the dish to a depth of about 1 inch (2.5 cm). Slide the rack into the oven, taking care not to slosh water onto the cake. Bake the cheesecake for 1 hour, then turn off the heat and leave the cake in the oven for another hour.

Remove the cake from the oven; cool to room temperature and then chill in the refrigerator for at least 6 hours. To remove the cake from the pan, gently run a knife around the perimeter of the cake, then release the spring, removing the pan side but leaving the pan bottom.

Place the cheesecake on a decorative serving platter and garnish the top with some red pepper slices and fresh cilantro leaves. To slice into neat portions, use a sharp knife rinsed under hot water between each cut. *Serves 12 to 16.*

Cherry pepper shooters

This fabulous appetizer is a classic Italian dish. It can be made with either hot or sweet cherry peppers.

24 ripe cherry peppers
1¼ cups (315 ml) white or red wine
⅓ lb (170 g) Monterey Jack cheese, or fine-quality mozzarella, cut in 1-in (2.5-cm) cubes
⅛ lb (65 g) prosciutto, thinly sliced and cut into strips

With a knife, cut off the top of each pepper. Using a melon baller or very small spoon, scoop out the seeds and pepper membranes.

In a saucepan, bring the wine to a boil. Add the peppers in two batches, poaching each batch for 1 minute. Drain the peppers cut side down on a paper towel.

Take a piece of cheese, wrap a tiny strip of prosciutto around it, and stuff it into a pepper. Repeat the process until all the peppers are stuffed. Place them on a platter and serve. *Serves 6.*

Deep-fried squash blossoms with chili cream

This recipe is from Michael Isles, chef-instructor. I worked with Michael when he was the chef at Mudd's Restaurant in San Ramon, California. The following Southwestern-style appetizer was a big hit with the patrons. The sauce can be used with other cooked vegetables, and served over grilled fish or poultry.

For the chili cream:
8 mild green 'Anaheim' chilies
1 red bell pepper
2 cups (500 ml) chicken stock
¼ cup (65 ml) heavy cream
Juice from ½ lime
Salt and pepper

For the squash blossoms:
12 squash blossoms
2 oz (65 g) pine nuts, chopped (about ½ cup)
4 oz (125 g) goat cheese
8 oz (250 g) natural cream cheese
2-in (5-cm) sprig fresh oregano, minced
⅛ teaspoon salt
⅛ teaspoon freshly ground black pepper
Flour for dredging
1 egg
½ cup (45 g) dried breadcrumbs
Peanut oil for frying
Garnish: fresh cilantro

To make the chili cream: Preheat the oven to 375°F (190°C). Roast the chilies and the bell pepper for 20 to 25 minutes. Place them in a paper bag to cool. Peel and seed the chilies and set them aside. Separately, peel and seed the bell pepper, dice, and set aside.

In a saucepan, bring the chicken stock to a boil. Add the roasted chilies, and simmer to reduce the liquid by one-quarter, stirring occasionally. Purée the mixture in a blender for about 45 seconds. Add the cream, the diced bell pepper, and lime juice to the purée. Season with salt and pepper to taste and set the cream aside.

To make the squash blossoms: Carefully examine the squash blossoms for critters and rinse out any you find. Remove the stamens because they could be bitter. In a dry cast-iron frying pan, toast the pine nuts over medium heat until barely golden, stirring to prevent burning.

In a small bowl, mix the cheeses, pine nuts, oregano, salt, and pepper. Fill a pastry bag with this mixture. One at a time, gently open the flowers and fill them with the cheese, leaving enough petal length to close the flower tightly.

Once all the blossoms are filled and closed, dredge each one lightly in the flour. In a small bowl, combine the egg with ¼ cup (65 ml) of water and mix them lightly. Dip the stuffed blossoms in the egg mixture, then drain and roll in enough breadcrumbs to coat them evenly, shaking off the excess.

Preheat the oven to 200°F (95°C). Using a large frying pan, pour in enough oil to cover the bottom to 2 inches (5 cm) deep. Heat the oil to 375°F (190°C) on a deep-frying thermometer. Deep-fry the stuffed blossoms a few at a time until they are golden brown. As they are done, drain each for a few minutes on a paper towel, then place them on a plate and put them in the oven to keep warm.

To serve, divide the cream sauce equally between 4 serving plates. Arrange 3 blossoms on each plate, garnish with cilantro, and serve immediately. *Serves 4.*

Gudi's potato pancakes with chives

In some parts of Germany these pancakes are made with grated onions. Here Gudi Riter, my kitchen assistant, used chives for a milder flavor and for their lovely green snippets of color. In Germany these pancakes are traditionally served with applesauce for a brunch or lunch. They are best eaten immediately out of the pan, when they are still hot and crisp.

2 lbs (1 kg) Yukon Gold or Yellow Fins potatoes, peeled
1 medium onion, peeled
$^1/_2$ cup (25 g) snipped fresh chives
2 eggs
3 tablespoons all-purpose flour
1 teaspoon salt
Freshly ground pepper and nutmeg
Vegetable oil
Garnish: chive blossoms

Finely grate the potatoes. (The best texture is achieved by using the second-smallest grater on a four-sided hand grater. The opening is less than $^1/_8$ inch/3 mm.) When grated, the potatoes will almost have the consistency of paste. Place the grated potatoes in a fine sieve or cheesecloth for about 15 minutes, to allow as much liquid as possible to drain. Squeeze the potatoes with your hands to extract more moisture if the mixture is still runny. (Some potatoes have more liquid than others.) When dry enough, the potato paste will more or less form a loose ball. Grate the onion using the same grater size.

In a mixing bowl, mix well the potato paste, grated onion, chives, and eggs. Add the flour, salt, pepper, and nutmeg to taste, and mix again.

In a large frying pan, add enough oil to cover the bottom of the pan to a depth of about $^1/_8$ inch (3 mm). Heat the oil over medium heat. With a tablespoon, put a generous dollop of batter into the pan and flatten it with the back of the spoon to about the size of the palm of your hand. Fry the pancakes, three or four at a time until golden brown on both sides (approximately 3 minutes per side). Remove the potato pancakes from the pan and drain them on paper towels. Serve immediately with a garnish of chive blossoms. *Makes 12 to 14 small pancakes. Serves 2 or 3 as a side dish, more as an appetizer.*

Edamame (fresh soybeans)

This recipe was suggested to me by June Tachibana, who sells fresh soybeans at the Palo Alto farmers' market. She says this traditional Japanese snack is often enjoyed with beer. Salt helps keep the soybeans bright green.

2 tablespoons salt
$^{1}/_{2}$ lb (250 g) fresh green soybeans, pods on

Pour 2 quarts (2 liters) of water in a large saucepan and bring it to a boil. Add the salt and stir to dissolve. Add the soybeans and boil them for 4 to 6 minutes until the beans are tender and still firm but not mushy. Drain the beans in a colander. Put the beans in a bowl and serve. Have snackers peel their own beans and provide them with an extra bowl for the empty pods. *Serves 2 as a snack.*

Mozzarella marinated with garlic, dried tomatoes, and basil

Arrive at a party with this lovely treat or serve it as an appetizer with focaccia or as part of an antipasto. Once the cheese and tomatoes have marinated, use the richly flavored olive oil for dressings or serve it with rustic bread for dipping. These mozzarella balls will keep in the refrigerator for about a week.

1 cup (55 g) dried tomatoes (see page 32)

³/₄ lb (340 g) fresh 1-in (2.5-cm) mozzarella balls

8 garlic cloves, minced, divided

1 teaspoon chopped fresh thyme, divided

1 teaspoon chopped fresh marjoram, divided

1 teaspoon whole green peppercorns or capers, divided

¹/₂ teaspoon salt, divided

¹/₄ teaspoon freshly ground black pepper, divided

Approximately 1¹/₄ cups (315 ml) extra-virgin olive oil

In a small bowl, pour 1 cup (250 ml) of boiling water over the dried tomatoes and let them sit for at least 15 minutes, or until they're soft. Drain them and set them aside.

Remove the mozzarella balls from the brine and drain them.

In a quart jar with a lid, layer half the tomatoes on the bottom, then make a layer using half the garlic, herbs, and seasonings. Layer all the mozzarella balls next. Make a top layer of the remaining tomatoes, then the remaining garlic, herbs, and seasonings. Pour the olive oil over the final layer, making sure to cover all the ingredients. Refrigerate to marinate for at least 24 hours. *Makes 1 quart (1 liter).*

Stuffed zucchini blossoms with goat cheese

You can't get too many zucchini blossom recipes and this elegant Italian-style appetizer takes advantage of the midsummer zucchini explosion.

3 tablespoons extra-virgin olive oil, divided
1 medium onion, chopped
2 garlic cloves, minced
1 medium red bell pepper, roasted, seeded, and chopped
8 large paste tomatoes (2 lbs/1 kg), peeled, seeded, and chopped
1 tablespoon tomato paste
1 teaspoon sugar
1 teaspoon balsamic vinegar
1/2 cup (125 ml) dry red wine
1/2 teaspoon chopped fresh thyme
1/4 cup (10 g) fresh basil, chopped
Salt and freshly ground black pepper to taste
8 small zucchini with their blossoms
6 oz (170 g) creamy-style goat cheese
2 tablespoons fresh basil, chopped
Garnish: fresh thyme leaves or chopped basil

Start by preparing the sauce. In a large saucepan heat 2 tablespoons of the olive oil and sauté the onions over medium heat until tender, about 7 minutes. Add the garlic cloves and sauté 4 minutes, or until they are soft but not brown. Add the bell pepper, tomatoes, tomato paste, sugar, and balsamic vinegar and simmer over low heat for about 45 minutes, or until the sauce is fairly thick, stirring occasionally. Add the wine, thyme, and basil and cook the sauce for 10 more minutes over medium heat. Press the sauce through a coarse sieve. You should have approximately 2 cups (500 ml) of sauce. Return the sauce to the saucepan, season it with salt and pepper, and set it aside.

Preheat the oven to 350°F (175°C). Carefully examine the zucchini blossoms for insects and remove the stamens and pistils. In a small bowl blend the goat cheese with 2 tablespoons of the basil. Fill each blossom with a scant tablespoon of the cheese. Try not to overstuff the blossoms or the cheese will ooze out as it cooks. Brush the bottom of a baking dish with 1 teaspoon of olive oil. Place the zucchini into the dish and drizzle them with the remaining olive oil. Bake them for 15 to 20 minutes, or until they are al dente and starting to brown, and the cheese has melted.

Warm the sauce and divide it equally among the plates. Spread the sauce to create a small pool on each plate and place the stuffed zucchini in the middle of the sauce. Garnish with herbs and serve. *Serves 8 as an appetizer, 4 as a side dish.*

Esquites (spicy corn kernels)

Kit Anderson bought this snacklike dish from a street vendor in Chapingo, Mexico, when she was visiting Professor Garrison Wilkes, a geneticist specializing in preserving corn varieties. She liked it so much we asked Professor Wilkes to track down the recipe. Esquites can be made with either field corn picked at the milk stage or with fresh, ripe sweet corn. In some versions, the corn is not fried in oil first, as it is here. Vendors sell it in cups with a spoon. See page 83 for tips on removing corn kernels from the cob.

3/4 cup (190 ml) oil or lard
1 medium onion, chopped
4 1/2 lbs (2.2 kg) corn kernels cut off the cobs
optional: 1/2 lb (250 g) longaniza sausage (found in Asian markets; substitute linguica)
2 to 5 serrano peppers, finely chopped, to taste
8 tomatillos, quartered
Half a handful epazote, chopped
1 to 2 tablespoons salt

Heat oil or lard in a large, heavy pot and sauté the onion. Add the corn, sausage, and chilies and fry over medium heat, stirring occasionally, until corn is slightly browned. Add the remaining ingredients and enough water to moisten slightly, cover, and simmer until corn is tender, 10 to 15 minutes. Makes enough for a fiesta.

Note: Epazote is a pungent herb shaped like a goosefoot, one of its common names. It is widely used in cooking in central and southern Mexico and the Yucatán. For aficionados, epazote is addictive and is indispensable in a bowl of black beans. While easily grown, it is sometimes difficult to find epazote in markets. It can be substituted with a combination of cilantro and lemongrass in many recipes.

Vegetable tempura

Tempura is a classic Japanese presentation and when done well is delightfully light and crunchy. Unlike most Japanese dishes, this is a meal that should be served piping hot. I've listed some of my favorite vegetables for tempura. Other vegetables, such as broccoli, yard-long beans, bell peppers, bamboo shoots, daikon radishes, and snow peas can also be used.

You will need a heavy deep pot for frying; a slotted spoon for lifting the fried foods out of the oil; a platter lined with paper towels to drain the fried vegetables; and a pair of long, wooden chopsticks (called cooking chopsticks) to dip the vegetables in the batter.

For the batter:

1 egg yolk
1 cup (250 ml) ice water
1 to 1¼ cups (100–120 g) sifted
    cake flour
1 pinch baking soda

For the tempura vegetables:

1 thin Japanese eggplant, sliced ⅛
    in (3 mm) thick
1 carrot, sliced into thin coins on the
    oblique
1 zucchini, sliced ¼ in (6 mm) thick
    on the oblique
½ sweet potato, peeled and sliced
    about ⅛ in (3 mm) thick
8 fresh, small button mushrooms
8 slices of winter squash, peeled
    and sliced about ⅛ in (3 mm) thick
Perilla leaves
Shungiku leaves (optional—see
    page 181 for more information)

For the dipping sauce:

1 cup (250 ml) commercial dashi (or
    make your own)
3 tablespoons soy sauce
3 tablespoons mirin
Pinch of salt

For the condiments:

½ cup (30 g) peeled, grated white
    daikon radish
2 teaspoons grated fresh ginger root
Lemon wedges

To make the batter: With a fork, combine the egg yolk with the ice water in a small bowl. The batter should be the texture of heavy cream, just thick enough to coat the vegetables. Just before frying the vegetables, stir in the flour and the baking soda, beating just long enough to combine without overworking the batter.

To make the tempura: The key to good tempura is as follows: use only fresh vegetable oil.

The oil should be at least 3 inches (8 cm) deep. The ideal frying temperature for vegetables is 320 to 340°F (160–170°C). To test, drop a bit of batter into the oil. It should drop to the bottom and then rise slowly to the surface. Be careful not to overheat the oil; if the oil smokes, it is too hot. Do not crowd the pot; for best results less than half the oil surface should be covered with vegetable pieces. Have all your ingredients at hand and arranged in the order that you will use them.

Preheat the oven to warm, about 200°F (95°C). To cook, coat each vegetable piece with the batter and fry for 1 minute. With the chopsticks turn the pieces and fry for another minute until the pieces are golden and puff up. Drain the vegetables on the paper towels and skim crumbs from the oil using a metal slotted spoon. Place the vegetable slices on a warm platter and keep them in the oven until you are done, or better yet, serve each piece to your guests as it comes out of the oil. Repeat the process with the other vegetables.

To serve the tempura: Make the sauce by heating the dashi, and then stirring in the soy sauce, mirin, and salt. As is traditionally done in Japan, provide each diner with a shallow bowl of the warm dipping sauce, to which they can add grated daikon and ginger to taste. Serve the tempura accompanied by the lemon wedges. *Serves 4.*

Salmon, cream cheese, and chive torta

This stylish dish is great for a Sunday brunch served with bagels or as part of a buffet accompanied by crusty bread. The final flavor and texture of the dish depend on using good natural cream cheese, with no added gums, and choosing flavorful smoked salmon.

1 lb (500 g) natural cream cheese
$^1/_2$ cup (25 g) plus 2 tablespoons snipped fresh chives
$^1/_2$ cup (70 g) finely chopped smoked Alaska wild salmon

Note: The best way to cut chives is to snip them with scissors. If you have extra chopped chives put them in a small self-sealing freezer bag and freeze them. They can be added directly to marinades and cooked dishes in the winter and won't need defrosting.

In a small bowl, crumble half of the cream cheese, add $^1/_2$ cup (25 g) of the chives, and mix together with a fork. If necessary, add a few teaspoons of water to hold the mixture together and make it spreadable. Do not make it too soft, or the torta will not hold its shape.

To shape the torta, drape a small piece of cheesecloth to line a $2^1/_2$- to 3-cup (625- to 750-ml) mold or straight-sided bowl. With a rubber spatula, form the bottom layer by spreading the chive and cream cheese mixture in the bottom of the mold, smoothing it out and filling any air holes.

In another bowl, crumble the remaining cream cheese and work in the salmon by repeating the procedure just outlined. Spread the salmon mixture on top of the chive mixture.

To unmold the torta, place a small serving plate facedown on top of the mold, making sure the cheesecloth is free of the plate and that the mold is centered on the plate. Hold the plate tightly against the top of the torta and turn the mold over. Lift off the mold and gently peel off the cheesecloth. To garnish, sprinkle the remaining 2 tablespoons of chives over the top. *Serves 6 to 8.*

Party spinach feta strudel

This traditional flaky Greek dish has been the star at many a party. If your filo dough is frozen, defrost it overnight in the refrigerator. Remove the filo dough from the refrigerator at least 3 hours before preparing the strudel.

2 lbs (1 kg) fresh spinach

¹/₃ cup (75 g) salted butter

1¹/₂ cups (230 g) finely chopped onions

5 eggs, slightly beaten

1 lb (500 g) feta cheese

1 cup (25 g) chopped fresh dill

¹/₄ cup (10 g) chopped fresh Italian parsley

¹/₄ teaspoon freshly ground black pepper

2 to 3 cups (4–6 sticks/460–675 g) unsalted butter

3 one-lb (500-g) packages of filo (strudel) dough

To prepare the filling: Wash the spinach well in two or three changes of water. Put 1 inch (2.5 mm) of water in the bottom of a steamer and bring it to a boil. Steam half the spinach until just wilted, remove, and put in a large bowl. Repeat this procedure with the rest of the spinach. Cool the spinach and by hand squeeze out most of the liquid, then coarsely chop.

Melt the salted butter in a frying pan over low heat. Add the onions and slowly cook until translucent, about 10 minutes. Add the onions to the spinach. Cool. Add the eggs, feta cheese, dill, parsley, and pepper and mix well. Chill for 30 minutes. If liquid collects, drain the mixture.

To assemble the pastries: Have on hand three cookie sheets, a damp, clean dish towel, and a pastry brush. In the microwave oven, melt the unsalted butter in a small bowl. When working with filo dough, never let it dry out. Cover it with a barely damp dish towel.

Lay one sheet of filo dough on a clean surface and lightly paint a thin layer of melted butter on it. Lay another sheet on top, repeating this process until you have created four layers. Paint the top layer with butter. Cut strips approximately 3 inches (8 cm) wide, cutting across the width (shortest dimension) of the layered filo. Place approximately 1¹/₂ teaspoons of spinach filling 1 inch (2.5 cm) in from the end of one strip. Fold a corner of the strip diagonally over the filling to form a triangle, then fold the triangle over itself all the way to the end, just as you would fold a flag. Brush it with butter and place it on a cookie sheet. (Your first few pastries will probably be uneven, but you'll soon perfect the technique.) Repeat with the remaining strips. Continue the layering procedure with the rest of the filo dough. Any leftover filling can be used to fill an omelet. (Pastries can be frozen at this point. Put them in the freezer on a cookie sheet lined with waxed paper. When they're completely frozen, transfer them to plastic freezer bags.)

Preheat the oven to 350°F (175°C). Bake for about 35 minutes, or until golden brown. Serve warm. *Makes about 60 (3-in/8-cm) pastries.*

Hearty vegetable dishes

Sunny delight squash blossom omelet

Squash blossoms can be combined with red peppers and yellow zucchini for a colorful and especially tasty dish. Choose from Sunny Delight, Gold Rush, Golden Dawn, Sunburst, and Yellow Crookneck yellow summer squashes for the brightest colors.

For the filling:

2 tablespoons extra-virgin olive oil

1 medium red onion, thinly sliced

1 garlic clove, minced

1 medium red bell pepper, seeded and chopped

6 baby yellow and green summer squash, cut in half lengthwise

6 large squash blossoms

2 tablespoons chopped fresh basil

$1/2$ teaspoon salt

Freshly ground black pepper

For the omelet:

6 large eggs

1 teaspoon olive oil

4 tablespoons grated Parmesan cheese

Garnish: 2 tablespoons snipped fresh chives and extra whole squash blossoms

To make the filling: In a large nonstick sauté pan, heat the olive oil and sauté the onions over medium heat until soft, about 7 minutes. Add the garlic and bell peppers and cook for 5 minutes or until tender. Remove the onion mixture to a bowl and set it aside. Put the yellow and green summer squash in the same pan and sauté them until lightly browned. Combine the onion mixture with the squash in the pan.

Carefully open the squash blossoms and remove any possible critters. Remove the stamens and pistils and coarsely chop the flowers. Add the chopped blossoms and the basil to the zucchini pan, season with the salt and pepper, cover, and set aside.

To make the omelet: In a small mixing bowl, mix 3 of the eggs using a fork. In a non-stick 8- to 10-inch (20–25-cm) sauté pan, heat the olive oil until hot, but not smoking. Pour the eggs into the pan (they should sizzle). Tilt the pan in a few directions to assure that the mixture evenly coats the pan. Give the mixture a gentle shake to make sure it is not sticking. With a spatula, gently lift sections of the cooked portions and let a little of the uncooked egg flow underneath.

When most of the egg is set but the top is still moist, sprinkle 2 tablespoons of the Parmesan cheese over one half of the omelet. Spoon half of the vegetable filling over the cheese. With a spatula make sure the omelet is not sticking and then gently fold the other half of the omelet over the filling.

Slide the omelet onto a preheated plate, garnish with the chives and squash blossoms. Repeat the process for the second omelet. *Serves 2.*

Huevos rancheros

This is my favorite breakfast. I find it works best to make the tomato sauce and refried beans the day before. Not only do they taste better but when I'm still sleepy, all I have to do is assemble the dish.

For the basic tomato sauce:
6 large paste tomatoes
1 medium white onion, quartered
2 cloves garlic, unpeeled
1 to 2 serrano peppers
1 tablespoon vegetable oil
1 teaspoon salt
¹/₂ teaspoon sugar
¹/₂ teaspoon Mexican oregano
Freshly ground black pepper to taste

For the huevos rancheros:
5 cups (1 kg) refried beans (see recipe, page 34)
1 to 2 tablespoons vegetable oil
8 corn tortillas
8 eggs
Salt and freshly ground black pepper to taste
Garnish: ¹/₄ cup (30 g) crumbled queso fresca, mozzarella, or Monterey Jack, and ¹/₄ cup (15 g) chopped cilantro

To make the basic tomato sauce: First, peel the tomatoes by putting a cross-slit at the base of each tomato and immersing it in boiling water to expand the skin. Then immerse it in ice water to contract the meat away from the skin. Discard the skin. On a hot comal or cast-iron frying pan, toast the onion, garlic, and serranos (see page 35). Peel the garlic and remove the seeds from the serranos and the tomatoes. Put all the vegetables into a blender and purée. In a saucepan, heat the vegetable oil. Carefully add the puréed vegetables, which will splatter. Add the salt, sugar, and Mexican oregano; simmer the sauce for about 20 minutes. If the tomatoes are very acidic, add more sugar; if they are sweet, omit the sugar. Season with freshly ground black pepper.

To make the huevos rancheros: Bring the tomato sauce and the refried beans to serving temperature and keep warm. Warm your serving plates. In a nonstick frying pan over medium heat, heat the oil and cook the tortillas, one at a time, for about 30 seconds each or until the tortilla starts to puff up and soften. Drain the tortillas on a paper towel and keep them in a warm oven. Fry the eggs in the remaining oil. To serve, put two tortillas on a plate; spread them with a generous amount of tomato sauce. Place the fried eggs on top of the tomato sauce. Serve about ³/₄ cup (190 g) refried beans for each diner. Sprinkle the eggs with salt, pepper, and cilantro. Garnish the beans with the crumbled queso fresca. *Serves 4.*

True-blue pancakes

These delicious, hearty pancakes get their lovely blue-green hue from the blue cornmeal and, of course, the blueberries.

³/₄ cup (85 g) all-purpose flour, sifted
2¹/₂ teaspoons baking powder
1 tablespoon sugar
1¹/₄ cups (375 g) blue cornmeal
³/₄ teaspoon salt
1 egg
1 cup (250 ml) milk
2 tablespoons vegetable oil
1 cup (150 g) fresh blueberries
Garnish: more fresh blueberries

In a medium bowl, put the flour, baking powder, sugar, cornmeal, and salt. Blend with a spoon. In another small bowl, put the egg, milk, and oil. Mix the wet ingredients with a spoon and pour them over the dry ingredients and lightly stir until the batter is just barely moist. Fold in the blueberries.

Heat a frying pan or griddle, lightly grease it, then cook 2 or 3 pancakes at a time over medium heat until both sides are golden brown and the insides are firm. Keep the pancakes warm in a low oven until all are cooked.

Stack the pancakes and serve them with maple syrup and more fresh blueberries. *Makes 8 to 10 three-inch (8-cm) pancakes.*

Strawberry french toast

This makes a very special Mother's Day brunch (it's lovely with champagne) and takes full advantage of a spring flush of berries.

For the filling:

1/4 lb (125 g) natural cream cheese
    (no gum added)
4 tablespoons strawberry yogurt
1 tablespoon powdered sugar
1 to 2 tablespoons milk
1 cup (170 g) sliced ripe strawberries

For the French toast:

4 eggs
1 cup (250 ml) milk
2 tablespoons sugar
1/2 teaspoon ground nutmeg
8 slices Italian bread, slightly stale
1 to 2 tablespoons unsalted butter
1 to 2 tablespoons vegetable oil
Garnish: whole strawberries

To make the filling: With an electric mixer, beat the cream cheese, yogurt, and powdered sugar until smooth and light. Slowly add the milk until the mixture is of spreading consistency. Gently fold in sliced strawberries. Cover with plastic wrap and set aside until the French toast is ready.

To make the French toast: In a shallow large bowl whisk eggs, milk, sugar, and nutmeg until blended. Soak the bread slices in this mixture for a few minutes. In a nonstick frying pan or griddle, over medium heat melt 1 tablespoon of butter. Add 1 tablespoon oil and stir to blend. Drain off any excess milk mixture from the bread slices as you remove them from the bowl and arrange them in one layer in the frying pan or griddle. Cook each slice until golden brown, turning occasionally for even browning. If you need to cook the toast in separate batches add more oil and butter for each batch and repeat the process. Keep the finished pieces warm in the oven.

Spread equal amounts of cream cheese onto 4 French toast slices and cover each with another slice of French toast, forming a sandwich. Place each serving on its own plate, cut it in half, and dust with powdered sugar. Garnish each plate with whole strawberries. *Serves 4.*

Savory bread pudding with sorrel and baby artichokes

This unusual and complex dish combines the nutty flavors of Swiss cheese and artichokes with the lightness of sorrel, interwoven with layers of fresh herbs. It can serve as the star of the meal served with an endive or beet salad and a good red wine, or accompany filets of salmon or tuna.

- 1 loaf of rustic Italian bread, or about 12 slices of leftover substantial breads of all types (avoid soft sandwich-type breads, since they tend to produce a gummy dish)
- 1 tablespoon fresh lemon juice
- 1 lb (500 g) 2-in- (5-cm-) long fresh or frozen baby artichokes (approximately 18)
- 3 cups (750 ml) nonfat or low-fat milk
- 5 eggs, beaten
- 1 teaspoon salt
- 1 teaspoon pepper
- 1/4 cup (25 g) grated Parmesan cheese, divided
- 4 oz (125 g) Monterey Jack cheese, slivered, divided
- 4 oz (125 g) Emmentaler cheese, slivered, divided
- 1 1/2 cups (60 g) chopped sorrel leaves
- 2 tablespoons snipped fresh chives
- 2 tablespoons chopped fresh Italian parsley
- 2 tablespoons chopped fresh lemon or English thyme
- 1 tablespoon butter, cut into small pieces

If you're using fresh bread, cut the loaf into 12 equal slices and arrange the slices on two cookie sheets. Bake at 200°F (95°C) for about 30 minutes, or until dry but not brown. Let the bread cool.

While the bread is in the oven, prepare the fresh artichokes. Partially fill a small bowl with water and add the lemon juice. Peel off any dried or bruised leaves from the artichokes, cut off the top 1/3 inch (1 mm) and discard it, and immediately immerse the artichokes in the lemon water to prevent them from turning brown. Place 1 inch (2.5 cm) of water in the steamer and bring it to a boil. Drain the artichokes and put them in the steamer basket, cover, and steam them over medium heat for about 20 minutes, or until they're just tender. Remove them from the heat and set them aside.

Break up the toasted bread slices and put them in a shallow baking dish. Pour the milk over the bread and let it soak for about 20 minutes, stirring the bread around to make sure it absorbs the milk and gets soft. After it has soaked, squeeze the milk out of the bread and set it aside. Pour the leftover milk into a measuring cup, adding more to get to 1/2 cup (125 ml) if necessary. In a bowl combine the 1/2 cup (125 ml) milk, eggs, salt, and pepper and mix well. Set aside.

Preheat the oven to 350°F (175°C). Oil a 3-quart (3-liter) casserole. Layer one-third of the bread in the bottom of the casserole. Layer two-thirds of the artichokes over the bread, then layer half of the three cheeses combined and then half the sorrel and herbs. Layer another one-third of the bread, add the final one-third of the artichokes (reserve a few for the top), the last half of the sorrel and herbs, and the rest of the cheeses, reserving 3 tablespoons for the top. Top the casserole with the last one-third of the bread and the reserved artichokes. Pour the milk and egg mixture over the bread, sprinkle on the reserved 3 tablespoons of combined cheeses, and dot with butter.

Bake for about 45 minutes, or until the top is nicely browned and a knife inserted halfway into the middle comes out clean. Serve hot. *Serves 4 as a hearty supper, 6 as a side dish.*

Spring pizza

Pizza can be made with dozens of different vegetables. This particular pizza includes traditional spring goodies—arugula and artichokes. I prefer a lesser amount of cheese, 6 ounces (180 g), for a lean pizza; other folks prefer their pizza "cheesy" and should use 8 ounces (250 g) of cheese.

4 baby artichokes

8 dried tomatoes

2 tablespoons extra-virgin olive oil

3 garlic cloves, minced

1 (12-in/30-cm) prebaked commercial pizza shell

6 to 8 oz (170–230 g) of fresh
mozzarella cheese, sliced thin

10 black, dried, piquées or kalamata
olives, pits removed

1 teaspoon fresh oregano, minced

1 cup (20 g) young arugula (rocket)
leaves

³/₄ cup (125 g) Asiago cheese, grated

Preheat the oven to 500°F (260°C). Cut the top ¹/₂ inch (13 mm) off the baby arti-chokes. Cover them with water and simmer them for 10 minutes, or until tender. Cool the artichokes.

While the artichokes are cooking, chop the tomatoes coarsely and reconstitute them in warm water for 10 minutes.

Blend the olive oil with the garlic. Spread the oil mixture evenly over the pizza shell. Distribute mozzarella cheese slices evenly over the pizza shell. Quarter the cooked artichokes and put them on top of the mozzarella. Add the olives and tomatoes and sprinkle them with the oregano. Bake the pizza for 7 to 10 min-utes, or until the cheese has melted. Remove it from the oven, cover it evenly with arugula, and sprinkle on the Asiago cheese.

Either serve the pizza as is or return it to the oven for 2 more minutes to wilt the arugula and melt the Asiago. *Makes 1 medium-size pizza that serves 2.*

Penne with arugula

This is a pasta dish with complexity and a full flavor. It can be served as a pasta course or a light supper.

2 tablespoons extra-virgin olive oil

2 portobello mushrooms, sliced
(about 2 cups/180 g)

3 garlic cloves, minced

6 thin slices (¹/₄–¹/₃ lb/125–170 g
total) prosciutto, chopped

4 paste tomatoes, peeled, seeded,
and chopped (about 2 cups/400 g)

4 cups (80 g) young arugula (rocket)
leaves

Freshly ground black pepper

4 cups (400 g) dried penne

4 tablespoons Asiago cheese, grated

In a deep frying pan, heat the olive oil and sauté the mushrooms over medium heat for 3 to 5 minutes, or until the mushrooms are lightly browned. Add the gar-lic and prosciutto and sauté for 2 more minutes. Reduce heat, add the tomatoes, and simmer for 1 more minute. Add the arugula and toss it in the pan until it has wilted, about 1 minute, then season with pepper.

Meanwhile, bring 3 quarts (3 liters) of salted water to a boil, add the penne, and cook until it's al dente, about 6 to 9 minutes. Drain the penne. In a warm bowl, toss the penne with the vegetables, and serve with grated Asiago cheese. *Serves 4 as a side dish.*

Fettuccine with fresh marinara sauce

This recipe calls for fettuccine, but any long noodle would work. The sauce is also great on polenta and grilled vegetables. Vary the herbs at whim—try any combination of parsley, tarragon, thyme, fennel, and anise seeds

For the sauce:
2 tablespoons extra-virgin olive oil
1 large onion, minced
3 garlic cloves, minced
1 bell pepper, roasted, peeled, and chopped
Approximately 20 paste tomatoes, blanched, peeled, seeded, and chopped (about 4 cups/800 g)
1 teaspoon chopped fresh Greek oregano
¼ cup (25 g) chopped fresh basil
Salt and freshly ground black pepper

For the noodles:
1 lb (500 g) dry fettuccine noodles
¼ lb (125 g) Parmigiano-Reggiano cheese (not grated)

To make the sauce: In a pan, heat the oil and sauté the onion until transparent, about 7 minutes. Add the garlic and sauté for 3 more minutes.

Add the bell pepper, tomatoes, oregano, and basil, lower the heat, and simmer for about 25 minutes, or until the mixture is fairly thick. Salt and pepper to taste. *Makes approximately 3½ cups (1 liter).*

To prepare the noodles: Boil 6 quarts (6 liters) of salted water. Add the fettuccine noodles and stir them for a few seconds to keep them separated. Boil the fettuccine until just barely tender, usually about 11 minutes. Drain the noodles in a colander and immediately pour them into a warm serving bowl. Pour on the warm sauce, toss, and serve immediately. Pass the cheese with a grater so diners can serve themselves. *Serves 6 to 8 for an Italian pasta course, or 4 to 6 as an American-style entrée.*

Pain bagna

Gudi Riter, my recipe consultant, fondly remembers having this type of crunchy, succulent sandwich at the beach when she vacationed in Provence as a teenager. If you don't have a pepper to roast or baby artichokes, substitute commercial roasted and peeled red peppers packed in olive oil and frozen or bottled marinated artichoke hearts. All are available from better grocery stores.

1 medium eggplant

2 tablespoons extra-virgin olive oil, divided

1 French baguette, crusty and rustic if possible

1 garlic clove

2 medium tomatoes, sliced

2 eggs, hard-boiled and sliced

$^1/_4$ small onion, thinly sliced

3 small artichoke hearts, sliced in half

1 red pepper, roasted, peeled, and sliced

1 two-oz (60-g) can anchovies

4 to 6 leaves from heart of romaine lettuce

8 fresh basil leaves

Freshly ground black pepper

Slice the eggplant and lightly rub it with some of the olive oil. Grill it on both sides over a medium fire for 3 to 5 minutes, or until it is slightly golden and tender. Remove it from the grill and set aside.

Cut the baguette into thirds and slice each piece in half lengthwise. Under a broiler or in a toaster oven, place the bread cut-side up and toast it just enough to warm it and get it slightly crisp, about 30 seconds. Rub the garlic clove over the cut side of each piece of bread. Drizzle the slices with some of the olive oil.

To assemble the sandwiches, place the bottom pieces of bread cut-side up and layer each with tomatoes, eggs, onion slices, artichokes, eggplant, peppers, anchovies, lettuce, and basil leaves. Grind black pepper over each open sandwich half and cover the layered half with its top. Press down to secure the top to the bottom and place on a serving plate. *Makes 3 sandwiches.*

Golden tomato tart

This spectacular tart can be served as an appetizer or as an entrée for a light lunch. It is quite dramatic made with gold tomatoes or any combination of colorful homegrown luscious tomatoes. Any leftover marinade can be used as a base for a vinaigrette dressing.

For the marinated tomatoes:

4 to 5 medium gold tomatoes, thinly sliced

6 to 7 gold cherry or pear tomatoes, halved

½ cup (125 ml) extra-virgin olive oil

1 to 2 garlic cloves, crushed

2 tablespoons chopped fresh parsley

1 tablespoon minced fresh chives

Freshly ground black pepper

For the filling:

1 cup (225 g) soft goat cheese or natural cream cheese

3 to 4 tablespoons heavy cream

1 tablespoon minced fresh rosemary

1 nine-in (23-cm) prebaked pie shell

Put both kinds of tomatoes into a bowl. In another bowl combine the ingredients for the marinade. Set aside ¼ cup (65 ml) of the marinade and pour the rest over the sliced tomatoes. Marinate them for at least 1 hour.

In a mixing bowl, combine the cheese with the cream and work them into a smooth, creamy consistency that will spread easily. Mix in the rosemary and spread the cheese mixture over the cooled pie crust.

Arrange the drained tomato slices in a single-layered circular pattern over cheese mixture, using the large slices for the outside and one slice for the middle. Fill in between the rows of large tomatoes with halved cherry tomatoes. Refrigerate until ready to serve. Just before serving, glaze the tomatoes with the remaining ¼ cup (65 ml) of the marinating mixture. *Serves 6 as an appetizer.*

Bean burritos

Burritos are popular in parts of northern Mexico and even more popular north of the border, especially at our house. The amounts in this recipe are a starting point—you'll probably never make them the same way twice.

For the guacamole:
1 large 'Hass' or 'Bacon' avocado
1 teaspoon lime juice
1 to 2 teaspoons chopped fresh cilantro
Pinch of salt
**Optional: 4 tablespoons fresh salsa
and two dried Mexican-type avocado
leaves, finely ground**

For the burritos:
1½ to 2 cups (380–500 g) refried beans
(see recipe on page 34)
½ to ¾ cup (80–120 g) roasted, peeled
poblanos cut in narrow strips or one
4-oz (125-g) can whole green chilies
4 burrito-size flour tortillas
½ to ¾ cup (125–190 ml) fresh salsa
(see recipe on page 127)
4 tablespoons guacamole
4 tablespoons sour cream
½ cup (60 g) grated jalapeño Monterey
Jack cheese
Cilantro

To make the guacamole: Peel the avocado, remove the seed, and mash the flesh. Add the lime juice, cilantro, salt, and optional salsa and avocado leaves, if using. Stir the mixture well. Makes about ½ cup (250 g).

To make the burritos: Heat the refried beans. In a separate pan, heat the chilies. Keep both warm. Heat the flour tortillas on a lightly greased nonstick frying pan or comal until warm and just starting to brown. Turn each one 2 or 3 times to keep them heating evenly. To keep them warm, place them, covered with a slightly damp tea towel, in a warm oven (200°F/95°C) until you are ready to assemble the burritos.

To assemble, place one flour tortilla on a clean work surface. Place a quarter of the beans in the center of the lower half of the tortilla. Place a quarter of the chilies on top of the beans. Sprinkle a few tablespoons each of salsa and cheese and 1 table-spoon each of guacamole and sour cream over the chilies. Add a few sprigs of cilantro, if you like. Fold the bottom up and the sides in, then roll to form a burrito. Serve with the remaining guacamole. *Serves 4.*

Note: Use only fresh flour tortillas. Don't let them dry out in the oven or the tortillas will crack when you try to roll them into a burrito.

Kaleidoscope tacos

These unusually colorful tacos are best served "do-it-yourself" style. Every diner assembles their own, according to taste. See page 83 for tips on removing corn kernels form the cob.

For the guacamole:
1 ripe avocado
1 teaspoon fresh lime juice
1 teaspoon sour cream
½ teaspoon chili powder

For the taco filling:
4 ears red or yellow sweet corn, husked
1 fifteen-oz (435-g) can black beans
½ lb (250 g) French feta cheese, sliced
1 yellow or orange bell pepper, sliced
6 leaves romaine lettuce, chopped
12 corn tortillas (one 14-oz/405-g package)

To make the guacamole: Cut the avocado in half; remove the pit and the peel. In a small bowl, mash the avocado with a fork, add the lime juice, sour cream, and chili powder. Mix until smooth and creamy. Place in a small bowl, cover with plastic wrap, and refrigerate until ready to serve.

To make the taco filling: Cook the ears of corn in the microwave on high for about 2 minutes each. With a sharp knife, cut off the kernels. Set them aside in a small bowl.

Drain the beans into a sieve; rinse them with cold water and set aside in a small bowl. Place cheese, peppers, and lettuce in separate bowls.

To make the tacos: Preheat the grill. Toast the corn tortillas on the hot grill for 10 to 20 seconds on each side. Present the guacamole, salsa, and the filling ingredients in bowls at the dining table.

Each diner should fill a tortilla with about 1 tablespoon each of guacamole, salsa, corn kernels, and the black beans, then add several small slices of feta cheese and bell pepper and the romaine and then fold them together to eat. *Serves 4.*

Note: Red seed corn is available from Burpee; the variety shown here is 'Ruby Queen.'

Onion tart

This classic dish blends the rich flavors of onions and butter. This onion tart is representative of the Alsace area of France. Slowly sautéing the onions is the secret to a rich flavor. Serve it as an appetizer or as an entrée with a soup or salad.

For the dough:

- 1 package (7 g) active dry yeast
- ½ teaspoon sugar
- ½ teaspoon salt
- 1 egg
- 3½ cups (390 g) of unbleached flour, divided
- 2 tablespoons butter, melted and cooled
- 1 egg yolk

For the onion filling:

- 2 tablespoons butter
- 4 to 6 medium yellow onions (about 6 cups/600 g), chopped
- 2 eggs
- 1 cup (250 ml) heavy cream
- 1 teaspoon (or more) caraway seeds
- Salt and freshly ground black pepper

To make the dough: In a large porcelain bowl dissolve the yeast in 1 cup (250 ml) lukewarm water. Add the sugar and salt. Beat in the egg. Add 1 cup (120 g) of the flour and beat the dough until it's smooth. Stir in the butter. Add the remaining 2½ cups (280 g) of flour to make a firm dough. Knead the dough until it's smooth and satiny, about 20 minutes by hand. Place the dough back in the bowl, sprinkle a little flour on top, cover with a clean cloth, and let it rise for 30 to 45 minutes, or until it has doubled.

When the dough has risen, punch it down and knead it briefly to remove any air bubbles. Let it rest for 5 minutes; then roll out into a rectangle, about ¼ inch (6 mm) thick, and place on an oiled cookie sheet. Form a ½-inch (13 mm) rim around the edge of the dough. Cover the dough with cloth and let it rise for another 10 minutes. Before baking, glaze the rim with egg yolk.

To make the onion filling: In a large saucepan melt the butter and stir in the onions, cover, and cook slowly for about 15 minutes, stirring occasionally until the onions look transparent. Cool the onions to room temperature. Add the eggs, cream, and caraway seeds; season with salt and pepper to taste.

Preheat the oven to 325°F (160°C).

Fill the dough shell with the onion mixture and bake for 20 to 30 minutes or until the top is set and golden brown. Serve hot or cold. *Serves 6 to 8 as an appetizer.*

Thai red vegetable curry

Red curry is one of the traditional dishes in Thailand. It is very spicy, and lush with coconut milk. Shrimp paste is available in Asian markets. Serve this curry over steamed rice.

For the red curry paste:

5 to 10 dried red chili peppers

1 tablespoon cumin seeds

1 teaspoon caraway seeds

20 whole black peppercorns

1 tablespoon whole coriander seeds

4 Kaffir lime leaves (fresh or dried)

3 shallots, minced

6 garlic cloves, minced

One 2½-in (6-cm) piece fresh ginger root, grated

2 stalks lemongrass, finely minced (white part only)

¼ cup (65 ml) vegetable oil

1 tablespoon fresh grated lime peel

1 tablespoon shrimp paste

For the vegetable curry:

3 carrots, peeled and thinly sliced

2 cups (120 g) snow peas, strings and stems removed

1 cup (60 g) peeled white daikon radish, cut into thin matchsticks

6 baby turnips

1 cup (175 g) broccoli, in small florets

2 cups (140 g) chopped Chinese cabbage

1 cup (70 g) tatsoi leaves

1 cup (70 g) chopped pac choi

1 cup (60 g) chopped mustard greens

¼ cup (65 ml) red curry paste (from above)

One 13.5-oz (400-g) can unsweetened coconut milk

2 teaspoons salt

1 tablespoon palm sugar or granulated sugar

4 tablespoons fresh lime juice

To make the red curry paste: Remove the stems and seeds from the chilies. Soak them in hot water for 15 minutes. Set them aside. In a dry cast-iron pan, toast the cumin seeds, caraway seeds, peppercorns, and coriander seeds over low heat until fragrant, about 3 minutes. Cool the spices and then grind together with the Kaffir lime leaves in a spice or coffee grinder until very fine.

Drain and chop the chili peppers. In a pan over low heat, sauté the chili peppers, shallots, garlic, ginger, and lemongrass in the vegetable oil until tender, about 5 minutes. Put the vegetables, ground spices, lime peel, and shrimp paste into the bowl of a food processor and process until you have a smooth paste, scraping down the sides once or twice. Stored in a sealed jar in the refrigerator, the paste keeps for about 3 weeks. *Yields 1 cup (250 ml).*

To make the vegetable curry: In a large pot, bring 2 quarts (2 liters) of salted water to a rolling boil. Add the carrots, snow peas, daikon, turnips, and broccoli and blanch for 2 minutes. Remove the vegetables with a slotted spoon, rinse them under cold running water to set the color and set them aside. Bring the water to a boil again and blanch the greens briefly. Drain and rinse them with cold water and set them aside with the other vegetables.

In a large pan, over low heat, sauté the curry paste for 3 minutes. Stir in the coconut milk, salt, palm sugar, and fresh lime juice. Heat the sauce but do not boil or it will curdle. Add the vegetables to the pan, toss together until well combined and adjust the seasoning. *Serves 4 to 6.*

Indonesian gado-gado

This is a classic Indonesian dish and has many variations. I like this one as it contains so many vegetables. It makes a wonderful vegetarian lunch.

For the sauce:

1 cup (250 g) chunky peanut butter

3 garlic cloves, minced

3 to 5 chilies, minced

2-in (5-cm) piece fresh ginger root, grated

$\frac{1}{3}$ cup (85 ml) soy sauce

1 teaspoon sugar

1 teaspoon salt

2 Kaffir lime leaves (fresh or dried)

4 tablespoons fresh lime juice

For the vegetables:

3 cups (500 g) yard-long beans, cut in 2-in (5-cm) lengths

3 medium carrots, cut into thin matchsticks

3 cups (225 g) fresh spinach, loosely packed

3 cups (250 g) chopped Chinese cabbage

2 cups (200 g) fresh bean sprouts

3 tablespoons vegetable oil

5 oz (150 g) firm tofu

$\frac{1}{2}$ medium onion, thinly sliced

4 hard-boiled eggs

To make the sauce: In a pot, combine the peanut butter, garlic, chilies, ginger, soy sauce, sugar, salt, lime leaves, and 2$\frac{1}{2}$ cups (625 ml) water. Bring the mixture to a boil and simmer, stirring often, for 30 minutes. Cool the sauce, stir in the fresh lime juice, and reserve.

To make the vegetables: In a large pot, bring 2 quarts (2 liters) of salted water to a rolling boil. Add the yard-long beans and carrots and cook them for 2 minutes. Remove them from the cooking water with a slotted spoon, rinse with cold water, and set them aside. Bring the water to a boil again and blanch the spinach, Chinese cabbage, and bean sprouts for 30 seconds. Drain and set aside.

To serve: In a frying pan, heat the vegetable oil and fry the tofu on all sides until golden brown. Drain on a paper towel and set aside. Add the sliced onions to the same pan and fry over medium heat until golden. Drain them on a paper towel and reserve. Quarter the hard-boiled eggs. Slice the tofu $\frac{1}{4}$ inch (6 mm) thick. In a serving bowl, toss the vegetables with the peanut sauce. Garnish with the sliced tofu, the quartered eggs, and the fried onions. *Serves 4 to 6.*

Stuffed red or yellow peppers

When one thinks of stuffed peppers, bell peppers usually come to mind. All large peppers can be used, however, with one caveat: some varieties have tougher skin than others, and diners may have to remove the skins as they eat. With one simple alteration, this dish can be made as spicy as you'd like. For extra hot, use a fiery habañero pepper in the filling. For a tamer version, choose a serrano or jalapeño pepper. If you don't like spicy foods, pick a mild poblano.

4 large or 6 medium red or yellow sweet peppers
6 ears white corn, shucked, or two 15-oz (430-g) cans of white corn
1 tablespoon extra-virgin olive oil
1 cup (100 g) sliced scallion (green onion)
2 garlic cloves, minced
2 cups (340 g) sliced mushrooms (about ²/₃ lb)
1 green bell pepper, diced
1 poblano, jalapeño, serrano, or habañero pepper (your choice: how spicy do you want them?)

2 teaspoons ground cumin
1¹/₂ tablespoons fresh oregano
1 teaspoon salt
Freshly ground black pepper to taste
3 cups (250 g) grated mozzarella cheese (¹/₂ lb)

Cut an opening into the side of each pepper and clean out the seeds and membranes. Elongated peppers should look like a canoe. Set them aside.

Preheat the oven to 325°F (160°C). Cut the kernels off the corn. You should have about 3 cups (870 g).

In a large saucepan, heat the olive oil, add the scallion, garlic, mushrooms, and peppers, and sauté for 10 minutes. Add the corn kernels, cumin, oregano, salt, and pepper, and cook for another 5 minutes. With a teaspoon, stuff the hollowed peppers. Place them close together in a greased baking dish. Sprinkle them with the mozzarella cheese and bake them for about 45 minutes. *Serves 4 to 6.*

Stir-fried japanese noodles

Noodles of many types are popular in Japan. I am most fond of the fresh noodles available in Asian grocery stores and usually keep some on hand. They are found in the refrigerator section and are sealed in plastic; they usually keep for a few months. Americans are most familiar with these ramen noodles in their dried form. The following is a much more satisfying dish than the dried commercial version and contains a lot more nutrition.

2 tablespoons corn oil
1/2 cup (70 g) chopped pickled mustard (see the recipe on page 31, or buy it from an Asian market)
1 cup (80 g) Chinese cabbage ribs, sliced
1 medium carrot, thinly sliced
1 large shallot or small onion, diced
4 cups (280 g) Chinese cabbage leaves, chopped

1 1/4 lbs (625 g) fresh Japanese noodles
1/2 cup (125 ml) chicken stock
1 tablespoon Worcestershire sauce
1/2 teaspoon chili powder
1/2 teaspoon sugar
1/2 teaspoon salt
Garnish: 1 sliced scallion (green onion)

In a wok, heat the corn oil over high heat. Add the pickled mustard, ribs of Chinese cabbage, and sliced carrots. Stir-fry for 2 minutes. Add the shallot and the chopped leaves of the Chinese cabbage and stir-fry 1 minute more. Toss in the noodles and cook for 2 more minutes. Add the chicken stock, Worcestershire sauce, chili powder, sugar, and salt. Cook 1 minute more to combine the flavors. Serve in a bowl garnished with sliced scallion. *Serves 2.*

Roasted pepper lasagna

This is a rich lasagna filled with great vegetables. All it needs is a loaf of good bread and a mesclun salad to create a feast.

For the lasagna noodles:
1 lb (500 g) dried lasagna noodles
1 tablespoon extra-virgin olive oil

For the filling:
1 lb (500 g) ricotta cheese
1 egg
3 garlic cloves, minced
1 tablespoon chopped fresh oregano
¼ cup (15 g) chopped fresh basil
    leaves
½ teaspoon hot pepper flakes
1 cup (90 g) grated parmesan cheese
6 pimiento peppers, roasted, peeled,
    and seeded
1 lb (500 g) fresh spinach, large
    stems removed
2 cups (230 g) mozzarella cheese,
    grated
3½ cups (875 ml) marinara sauce

For the béchamel sauce:
2 tablespoons butter
3 tablespoons flour
2 cups (500 ml) milk
Pinch of freshly grated nutmeg
Salt and freshly ground black pepper

To cook the lasagna noodles: In a large pot of boiling salted water, cook the lasagna noodles for 9 minutes or until just tender. Drain them and separate them. Brush each lasagna noodle lightly with olive oil so they will not stick together. Set them aside.

To make the filling: In a small bowl, blend the ricotta with the egg, garlic, oregano, basil, hot pepper flakes, and 2 tablespoons of the Parmesan cheese and set aside.
    Slice the roasted pimiento into strips 2 inches (5 cm) wide and set aside.
    Wash the spinach. Steam the spinach until wilted, about 1 minute. Squeeze out some of the liquid and set the spinach aside.

To make the béchamel sauce: Melt the butter in a heavy saucepan. Using a wire whisk, stir in the flour. Add the milk a little at a time, while stirring. Simmer over low to medium heat until the sauce thickens, stirring constantly to avoid lumps and burning. Once the sauce thickens, cook it for 1 minute longer. Season the sauce with nutmeg, salt, and pepper.

To assemble the lasagna: Preheat the oven to 350°F (175°C). Brush the bottom of a large (14 x 9 x 2 in/35 x 25 x 5 cm) baking dish with the olive oil. Cover the bottom of the dish with a single layer of lasagna noodles. Spread the ricotta mixture over the noodles.
    Cover the ricotta with the pepper slices and sprinkle with ½ cup (60 g) mozzarella. Cover with a layer of noodles. Spread the spinach over the noodles and cover with the béchamel sauce and ½ cup (60 g) more of mozzarella. Cover with a last layer of noodles, and sprinkle them with another ½ cup (60 g) of mozzarella.
    Pour the marinara sauce over the lasagna. Sprinkle it with the remaining mozzarella and parmesan cheese. Bake the lasagna for 30 to 40 minutes or until the cheese is lightly browned and bubbly. Let the lasagna sit for about 10 minutes so the juices will be absorbed before serving. Cut in serving-size squares.
Serves 6 to 8.

Zucchini pancakes with tomato salsa

Most often, I serve these pancakes with salsa for a light supper; but for breakfast I omit the onions and serve them with maple syrup. This is a fun dish to make with children. If they want to do it all by themselves, a package of corn muffin mix works well. Follow the directions for cornmeal pancakes and add the vegetables to the wet mixture.

For the salsa:

2 **yellow or orange tomatoes, chopped**

2 **tablespoons chopped red onion**

1 **small avocado, peeled, pitted, and chopped**

1 **teaspoon minced jalapeño pepper**

1 **tablespoon minced fresh cilantro**

2 **tablespoons fresh lime juice**

2 **tablespoons extra-virgin olive oil**

$^1/_4$ **teaspoon ground cumin**

$^1/_8$ **teaspoon salt**

Freshly ground black pepper

For the pancakes:

$^3/_4$ **cup (85 g) all-purpose flour, sifted**

2$^1/_2$ **teaspoons baking powder**

1 **tablespoon sugar**

1$^1/_4$ **cups (190 g) yellow cornmeal**

$^3/_4$ **teaspoon salt**

1 **egg**

1 **cup (250 ml) milk**

2 **tablespoons vegetable oil**

1 **cup (175 g) grated yellow summer squash or yellow zucchini (about 1$^1/_2$ medium)**

3 **tablespoons yellow bell pepper, seeded and chopped fine**

3 **tablespoons finely chopped onion**

1 **cup (250 ml) fresh salsa (from above), or your favorite commercial salsa**

To make the salsa: In a bowl, combine the tomatoes, red onion, avocado, jalapeño pepper, and the cilantro with the lime juice, olive oil, cumin, and salt and pepper. Cover with plastic wrap and set aside.

To make the pancakes: In a medium bowl, put flour, baking powder, sugar, cornmeal and salt. Blend with a spoon. In a small bowl, put the egg, milk, oil, squash, pepper, and onion. Mix the wet ingredients with a spoon. Pour over the dry ingredients and stir lightly until just barely moist.

Heat a nonstick frying pan or griddle, then cook 2 or 3 pancakes at a time over medium heat until both sides are golden brown and the insides are firm. Keep the pancakes warm in a low oven until all are cooked. Serve the pancakes with the salsa. *Makes 8 to 10 three-inch (8-cm) pancakes.*

Quesadillas

Traditional quesadillas are corn tortillas or masa folded over a cheese filling and fried. Sometimes chopped and cooked prickly pear cactus paddles or squash blossoms are added. In the Southwest, the concept has expanded, and some families (like mine) eat quesadillas day and night as either a snack or light meal and make them with both the traditional corn tortillas and flour tortillas. I find it easier to cook a sandwich quesadilla, with a bottom and a top tortilla, than the traditional folded-in-half tortilla. It's easier to manage on the comal and I can use less-than-fresh tortillas because stale ones crack when folded.

4 corn tortillas
½ to ⅔ cup (60–80 g) crumbled queso fresca or grated plain or hot pepper Monterey Jack cheese
½ cup (70 g) roasted poblano peppers cut into thin matchsticks or canned, chopped hot peppers
Cilantro

Heat a comal, well-seasoned cast-iron frying pan, or nonstick sauté pan over fairly high heat. Place two tortillas on a clean, dry surface. Sprinkle half of the cheese, half of the chili strips, and a few leaves of cilantro on each tortilla. Cover each with another tortilla. Put 1 filled tortilla sandwich on the comal. Press down occasionally with a spatula. When the cheese melts, you can turn the tortilla sandwich over without it coming apart; turn and cook the other side until it starts to get slightly golden in spots. Turn it back over and cook until the first side is slightly golden as well. Transfer the quesadilla to a warm serving plate and repeat the process with the second quesadilla. Cut each quesadilla into 4 ple-shaped wedges. Serve with salsa and/or guacamole in which to dip the quesadillas. (See pages 127 and 118 for recipes.) *Serves 1 for lunch.*

Mexican-style pizza with cilantro

Paste tomatoes are best for this recipe as their meaty fruits won't make your pizza soggy. This unusual pizza marries the best Southwestern seasonings with Italian basics. It's dynamite!

1 tablespoon extra-virgin olive oil

1 medium onion, sliced

3 large cloves garlic, pressed, divided

1 uncooked 10-in (25-cm) pizza shell, your own or a commercial one

$^1/_3$ lb (1$^1/_4$ cups/170 g) grated Monterey Jack cheese

1 to 6 teaspoons minced jalapeño peppers, to taste

2 medium paste tomatoes, sliced

Freshly ground black pepper to taste

3 to 4 finely chopped tablespoons of fresh cilantro

$^1/_3$ teaspoon cumin seeds

Preheat the oven to 400°F (200°C). Heat a medium frying pan and add the olive oil. Add the onions and two cloves of pressed garlic and sauté over medium heat until the onion is soft and translucent, about ten minutes.

Place the pizza shell on a baking sheet. Distribute the cheese evenly over the pizza shell, reserving about $^1/_2$ cup (60 g) of cheese for the top. Spread the sautéed onion and garlic mixture and jalapeño peppers over the cheese. Slice the tomatoes and place on top of the cheese and onions. Grind black pepper over the tomatoes. Mix the chopped cilantro with the remaining clove of pressed garlic and distribute this mixture over the pizza. Sprinkle the cumin seeds and the reserved $^1/_2$ cup (60 g) of cheese over the pizza.

Bake for approximately 20 minutes or until the cheese is bubbling and the crust is light brown. Cut pizza into 8 slices and serve immediately. *Serves 4.*

Technicolor nachos

Tortilla chips and peppers come in many colors. This recipe is a variation on a tried-and-true restaurant dish.

For the salsa:

2 to 4 fresh serrano or jalapeño peppers
½ medium white onion, minced
2 cloves garlic, pressed or minced
4 large, ripe tomatoes, minced and seeded
3 tablespoons fresh minced cilantro
Salt to taste

For the nachos:

12 oz (340 g) corn tortilla chips (red or blue or a combination of both)
1 lb (450 g) of pepper Jack cheese, grated
1½ cups (180 g) roasted pepper strips, of all different colors
1 teaspoon ground cumin
Garnish: 2 tablespoons freshly chopped cilantro

To make the salsa: Stem the chilies (seed, too, if you desire a milder salsa) and then mince. Combine them with the remaining ingredients.

To make the nachos: Preheat the oven to 350°F (175°C). Place one layer of chips in a baking dish. Sprinkle with ⅓ of each of the cheese, the pepper strips, and the cumin. Repeat with a second and third layer. Bake until the cheese has melted and started to brown, about 3 to 5 minutes. Watch carefully to avoid burning the chips. Garnish the nachos with the cilantro and serve with the salsa. *Serves 4.*

Fennel rice with pistachios

This "fragrantly" flavorful dish makes a wonderful accompaniment for fish or roasted chicken, or you can add grated cheese before you cover the rice with the bread-crumb mixture for a vegetarian main course. I prefer to use Carolina or Basmati rice as they have a light, rich texture.

2 cups (450 g) uncooked white long-grain rice

4 1/2 cups (1.2 liters) vegetable broth, divided

1 bay leaf

2 Florence fennel bulbs (3–4 in/8–10 cm wide) with greens (approximately 2 lbs/1 kg)

2 tablespoons olive oil

1 large onion, coarsely chopped

2 garlic cloves, minced

1 teaspoon fennel seeds

1 teaspoon coriander seeds

2 tablespoons chopped fresh parsley

Salt and freshly ground black pepper to taste

1 cup (95 g) grated Gruyère cheese (optional)

1 1/2 cups (75 g) fresh breadcrumbs

1/3 cup (30 g) chopped shelled pistachio nuts or shelled almonds

1/8 teaspoon freshly ground black pepper, plus extra

1 tablespoon butter, melted

Place the rice in a large saucepan or rice cooker. Add 3 1/2 cups (875 ml) of the vegetable broth and the bay leaf. Bring it to a boil, then cover and cook over low heat for about 20 minutes, or until the rice is tender and the liquid has been absorbed. Remove the bay leaf.

Meanwhile, remove the fennel leaves from the stems, setting aside a few leaves for a garnish. Finely chop the leaves. Cut the fennel bulbs crosswise into fine dice.

In a large frying pan, heat the olive oil over medium heat. Add the onions, garlic, and diced fennel bulbs and sauté, stirring occasionally, for about 10 minutes, or until translucent.

With a blender or mortar and pestle, coarsely grind the fennel seeds and coriander seeds.

In a large bowl, combine the onion mixture, cooked rice, chopped fennel greens, parsley, and the ground coriander and fennel seeds. Add salt and pepper to taste. (At this point you could stir in the nuts and serve immediately as a simple side dish.)

Preheat the oven to 350°F (175°C). Grease a 3-quart (3-liter) shallow ovenproof casserole dish. Add the remaining vegetable broth to the rice and mix. Spread the rice mixture evenly in the dish. Sprinkle grated Gruyère cheese over the rice, if desired. In a small bowl, combine the breadcrumbs, nuts, and the 1/8 teaspoon of black pepper. Sprinkle the breadcrumb mixture over the rice. Drizzle melted butter on top. Bake for about 15 minutes, or until the top is a light golden brown. Serve garnished with fennel leaves. *Serves 6.*

Delicious meat,
poultry, and
seafood dishes

Vietnamese salad rolls

This elegant recipe is a fabulous way to feature Southeast Asian herbs. It is a traditional dish and was given to me by Mai Truong, who grew up in Vietnam. It makes a great light first course or a special luncheon dish. Use leftover fish dipping sauce for a light salad dressing.

For the salad rolls:

1 lb (500 g) pork loin (or use left-over roasted or grilled pork loin)

16 to 20 medium raw shrimp

6 oz (200 g) fine rice vermicelli

1 large head leaf or butter lettuce

5 to 6 cups (250–300 g) loosely packed fresh herb leaves including: mint, Thai basil, perilla leaves, Vietnamese coriander (rau ram), and cilantro

2 cups (200 g) mung bean sprouts

1 twelve-oz (340-g) package of 11-in (28-cm) egg roll wrappers (made with wheat flour, tapioca, and water)

1 large bunch garlic chive leaves

1 tablespoon hot chili paste

For the hoisin dipping sauce:

½ cup (125 ml) hoisin sauce

2 tablespoons water

1 tablespoon unsalted, dry-roasted peanuts, finely chopped

For the fish dipping sauce:

3 to 6 garlic cloves, minced

3 fresh serrano peppers, seeded and minced

¼ cup (65 ml) fresh lemon juice

⅓ cup (85 ml) Vietnamese fish sauce (nuoc nam)

¼ cup (60 g) sugar

To make the salad rolls: In a saucepan, bring 1 quart (1 liter) of water to a boil. Add the pork loin; cover and simmer on low heat for about 20 to 30 minutes or until tender. Drain and cool the pork. In another saucepan, bring 2 cups (500 ml) of water to a boil, add the shrimp and simmer on low for about 3 minutes. Drain and set them aside. In a third pot, bring 1 quart (1 liter) of water to a boil, add the vermicelli and cook for 3 minutes. Drain, rinse in cold water, and set aside.

Before assembling the rolls, cut the pork into thin slices. Peel and devein the shrimp and slice each in half lengthwise. Wash and drain the lettuce and herbs. Place the pork, shrimp, vermicelli, lettuce leaves, herb leaves, and bean sprouts in bowls near a clean work surface.

Fill a large bowl with warm water and keep it at your work table. Dampen one egg roll wrapper at a time by dipping the edges into the warm water; place it on your work surface and dampen the middle by sprinkling it with water. Spread the moisture around with your fingers so the wrapper becomes evenly moist, but not wet. Let the wrapper soften a few seconds. (The thickness of the salad rolls can vary—it depends on how much filling you put in. After you fill and roll a few you will determine the final size you prefer.)

To fill the first wrapper, spread several strands of noodles on it, 2 inches (5 cm) from the bottom. Cover with part of a lettuce leaf, a selection of 3 or 4 different herb leaves, a small amount of bean sprouts, and three slices of the pork on top of each other. Fold the bottom part of the wrapper over the ingredients and fold in both sides of the wrapper, as you would to make a burrito. Place 3 shrimp halves and 3 whole garlic chive leaves on the top of the first roll of the wrapper, letting the chives stick out on one side. Finish rolling the wrapper up until it forms a cylinder. The shrimp will be visible from the outside through the wrapper. Repeat assembly for each roll.

Top left: To roll the salad rolls, first place the ingredients on the damp wrapper a few inches from the bottom. **Bottom left:** Fold the bottom part of the wrapper over the ingredients, then bring over the sides. Place 3 shrimp in front of the rolled part and roll a half turn. **Top right:** Place a few chive leaves on the wrapper, then roll another turn until the roll is finished (**bottom right**).

Place the finished rolls on a serving platter and garnish, or make up individual plates of 2 or 3 rolls each. Accompany the rolls with a small bowl of hoisin dipping sauce, another small bowl of fish dipping sauce, and a bowl of the hot chili paste. *Makes 10 to 12 rolls, serves 4 to 6.*

To make the hoisin sauce: Blend the hoisin sauce with the water. Put it in a small serving bowl and sprinkle with the chopped peanuts.

To make the fish dipping sauce: With a mortar and pestle, crush the garlic and peppers into a smooth paste. Put the lemon juice into a glass bowl, add the garlic-pepper paste, fish sauce, sugar, and 3/4 cup (190 ml) warm water. Stir to combine. This dipping sauce can be kept in a jar in the refrigerator for several weeks. *Makes 1 1/2 cups (375 ml).*

Pork shoulder sandwiches with tomatillos

These sandwiches are variations on ones shown to me by Luis Torres and his sister Virginia Vasquez. Virginia's brother-in-law, Javier Vasquez, who sold similar tortas from his food stand in Guadalajara, Mexico, was the original inspiration. The best way to describe these sandwiches is as sloppy joes with a south-of-the-border flavor.

For the meat filling:

5 lbs (2.5 kg) fresh pork shoulder
5 to 8 dried bay leaves (or 8 fresh bay leaves)
½ tablespoon whole cloves
1½ tablespoons vegetable oil
1 large white onion, chopped finely
4 cups (530 g) finely chopped tomatillos
2 large tomatoes, chopped finely
1 seven-oz (220-g) can chipotle en adobo (the amount you use depends on how much heat you want)
1 teaspoon cumin seeds
¼ teaspoon ground cloves
Salt to taste

To make the meat filling: Cut the pork off the bones into pieces approximately 2 x 3 inches (5 x 7.5 cm). Remove large pieces of fat but retain the bones. In a 12-quart (12-liter) kettle, put 2 quarts (2 liters) of water and bring to a boil. Tie the bay leaves and cloves in cheesecloth. Put the pork, the bones, and the cheesecloth bag into the boiling water. Simmer the pork for 2 hours, uncovered for the first hour, covered for the second hour, until it is very tender and shreds readily.

In the meantime, over medium heat, in a large frying pan, heat the oil; add the onions and sauté them for about 6 minutes or until they are translucent and just starting to brown. Add the tomatillos and sauté for about 5 minutes, then add the tomatoes and simmer for 10 minutes or until they are tender.

Heat a dry frying pan and toast the cumin seeds for a minute or so until they start to perfume the air. Grind the seeds in a spice grinder or mortar and pestle. In a blender, put the chipotle en adobo, the ground cumin, and the ground cloves. Add ½ cup (125 ml) of the pork cooking liquid and blend until smooth. Add the chipotle mixture to the tomatillo mixture and cook over medium heat, stirring, for about 5 minutes.

For the sandwich:

1 large white onion, thinly sliced
Juice of ¼ lime
8 to 12 bolillo (Mexican rolls) or 6-in (15-cm) French sandwich rolls
8 tablespoons butter (1 stick)
6 medium tomatoes, sliced
1 head iceberg lettuce, thinly sliced
1 cup (230 g) Mexican crema or sour cream

When the pork is tender, drain it into a colander, saving the broth (you should have between 2 and 3 cups [500–750 ml] of broth). If you like your sandwiches especially sloppy, keep the 3 cups (750 ml); if you prefer them a little drier, boil the liquid down to 2 cups (500 ml).

Remove the bag of spices and the bones and discard them. Put the meat into a large bowl and cool. With your fingers, pull the meat into shreds; this can also be done with a potato masher. Return the reserved broth to the pot. Add the meat and the tomatillo mixture to the broth and bring it back to a simmer. Once hot, prepare the sandwiches or refrigerate and reheat to serve the next day.

To make the sandwich: Put the onion slices in a small bowl and marinate them in the lime juice for 20 minutes. Cut the rolls lengthwise until nearly halved. Liberally butter the rolls and toast them on a medium to hot comal or grill until they are quite brown. Make them into sandwiches with dollops of warm pork mixture, sliced onion, tomato, lettuce, and crema to taste. Add mariachi music and enjoy! *Serves 8 to 10.*

Gardener's spring lamb

Georgeanne Brennan, author of *Potager*, contributed this recipe, which is called *navarin printanier* in French. She drew upon her years in France to create it.

2 lbs (1 kg) boned shoulder of lamb
Salt and freshly ground black pepper
2 tablespoons butter
1 tablespoon extra-virgin olive oil
2 tablespoons all-purpose flour
3 to 4 cups (750 ml–1 liter) beef stock, divided
2 garlic cloves
4 sprigs fresh parsley
4 sprigs fresh chervil (optional)
2 fresh bay leaves
16 very small new potatoes
16 small (2-in-/5-cm-long) new carrots
12 small new turnips
16 small onions, or 8 new shallots or 16 scallions (green onions)
2 cups (300 g) shelled peas (preferably *petit pois*)

Cut the lamb into ½-inch (13-mm) cubes. Toss with salt and pepper and set aside for an hour or so.

In a heavy casserole, melt the butter and add the olive oil. Brown the lamb over high heat; then remove it to a platter. Off heat, stir the flour into the pan juices in the casserole to make a thick paste. Return the casserole to the heat, and over high heat gradually add half the beef stock, stirring constantly. When the sauce is smooth, add the garlic, parsley, chervil, and bay leaves. Add the lamb, cover, and simmer for 1 hour.

Meanwhile, peel the potatoes, carrots, and turnips but leave them whole. Peel the onions (if you're using scallions, peel them, trim the roots, and cut off the tops, leaving only the white plus 1 inch/2.5 cm of green). Add the potatoes, carrots, turnips, and onions to the casserole and cook for 45 minutes, uncovered. Skim any surface fat or foam. Add the peas and continue cooking until they are tender, about 5 minutes. Serve in a hot dish. *Serves 4 to 6.*

Beef and pork japanese vegetable rolls

The Japanese have many elegant meat and vegetable combination dishes and this is one.

For the sauce:
¼ cup (65 ml) water
1 tablespoon sugar
1 tablespoon mirin
3 tablespoons soy sauce

For the rolls:
2 medium carrots (about 4 oz/125 g)
1 burdock root (about 4 oz/125 g) (optional)
1 tablespoon white vinegar
6 scallions (green onions)
4 oz (125 g) yard-long beans
1 teaspoon soy sauce
10 oz (390 g) lean beef or pork, teriyaki-style, and thinly sliced
2 tablespoons cornstarch
1 tablespoon vegetable oil

To make the sauce: Combine the water with the sugar, mirin, and soy sauce and set aside.

To make the rolls: Cut the carrots lengthwise into strips about 5 inches (13 cm) long and ¼ inch (6 mm) square. Peel the skin off the burdock root and cut it into the same size strips as the carrots. If using the burdock, to prevent discoloration soak it in water with the vinegar for 5 minutes. Cut the scallions and set them aside. Cut the yard-long beans into 5-inch (13-cm) lengths.

In a small saucepan, bring ¼ cup (65 ml) water to a boil, add 1 teaspoon soy sauce, the carrots, and the burdock root. Simmer the vegetables for 5 minutes, drain them, and set aside. Parboil the beans in 2 cups (500 ml) of water for 3 minutes, cool them quickly under

running cold water, drain them, and set them aside.

Spread the beef or pork slices on a cutting board and sprinkle them lightly with cornstarch.

To assemble: Put 2 pieces of each vegetable and scallions on a piece of meat and roll them up tightly. Secure the rolls with a wooden toothpick. When all the rolls are done, sprinkle them lightly with cornstarch.

To serve: In a nonstick frying pan, heat the vegetable oil and brown the rolls evenly on all sides. You may have to do this in 2 batches. Return all the rolls to the pan and pour the sauce over the rolls and simmer them for another 5 minutes, turning them in the sauce so they are evenly glazed. Serve on individual plates while still warm. *Serves 4.*

Pork stew with purslane

This is a classic Mexican recipe. Prickly pear cactus paddles or chard can be used instead of the purslane and pork short ribs for the pork loin. Serve the stew with corn tortillas and, for garnishing, fresh salsa, chopped cilantro, and Mexican crema, if you choose. Leftover stew is great the next day served with warm tortillas.

For the sauce base:
1 lb (500 g) tomatillos, husked
2 to 4 serrano peppers
1 small white onion, quartered
2 cloves garlic, unpeeled
¹/₂ cup (250 ml) beef broth
¹/₂ cup (25 g) cilantro, chopped
Salt to taste

For the stew:
2 tablespoons vegetable oil
1¹/₂ lbs (725 g) pork loin, cubed
1 medium white onion, finely chopped
1 clove garlic, minced
6 Yukon gold or red boiling potatoes, peeled and quartered
3 cups (130 g) purslane shoots, thick stems removed (usually grows in cultivated fields, and is more likely found at a farm stand or Mexican market than at the supermarket)
1 teaspoon dried Mexican oregano
Salt to taste
Garnish: chopped cilantro

To make the sauce base: On a hot comal or cast-iron frying pan, toast the tomatillos, serranos, onions, and garlic until brown. Remove the seeds from the serranos and the skin from the garlic. In a blender, purée the toasted vegetables with the beef broth until smooth. Add the chopped cilantro and salt, stir, and set aside.

To make the stew: Preheat the oven to 325°F (160°C). In a heavy-bottomed ovenproof pot with a cover, or a Dutch oven, heat the oil. Add the pork and brown over medium heat, about 15 to 20 minutes. (You probably need to do this in at least 2 batches.) Remove the meat from the pot and set aside. Sauté the onions and garlic in the same pot over low heat until tender. Add the tomatillo sauce base and bring it to a rolling boil; add the meat, cover the pot, and bake in the oven for 30 minutes. Add the potatoes, cover, and bake for 20–30 more minutes or until the potatoes are tender. Add the purslane and cook 5 minutes more. On a hot comal or dry frying pan, toast the Mexican oregano for about 30 seconds; cool and crumble. Season the stew with the oregano and salt. Serve with the chopped cilantro. *Serves 4.*

V.O.M.
CHILI
COOK OFF

Garden fresh chili

Making this chili, full of lively fresh flavors and colors, is a festive way to celebrate the late-summer harvest. Be creative and flexible and use the vegetables and herbs your garden offers. For a vegetarian version, omit the meat and double the quantity of beans and garlic. Serve with corn bread and a green salad.

½ lb (250 g) dry beans (recommended: pinto, kidney, or red Mexican; about 1¼ cups) or 2 to 3 cups (380–580 g) fresh shelled beans (omit precooking)
¼ cup (65 ml) extra-virgin olive oil
2 onions, chopped
1 lb (500 g) chuck roast or steak, cut into ½-in (2.5-cm) cubes
4 garlic cloves, minced
1 or 2 chili peppers, minced
3 tablespoons chili powder
2 teaspoons cumin

2 quarts (1.5 kg) tomatoes, peeled and seeded (about 8 medium tomatoes)
1 or 2 sweet peppers, diced
2 small or 1 large summer squash (recommended: 1 each yellow and green zucchini), diced
¾ cup (130 g) fresh corn kernels (cut from 1 ear)
1½ tablespoons minced fresh oregano
¼ cup (10 g) minced fresh basil or parsley

Cover the dry beans generously with water and soak overnight. Before cooking, add more water if needed to cover beans and simmer 1½ to 2½ hours or until just tender.

In a large kettle, sauté the onions in olive oil until soft. Add the meat, garlic, chili peppers, chili powder, and cumin, and sauté for about 4 minutes.

Add the tomatoes, cover the kettle, and simmer about 1 hour, stirring occasionally. Add the remaining vegetables, the herbs, and the cooked dry beans (or fresh shelled beans, if used) and simmer ½ hour longer. *Serves 8 to 10.*

Black bean and chicken chili

This recipe was contributed by Jesse Cool, owner and chef at Flea Street Café in Menlo Park, California. You'll be amazed at all the rich flavors.

2 cups (400 g) dry black beans
2 lbs (1 kg) meaty chicken (breasts and/or thighs)
Salt and pepper
¼ cup (65 ml) olive oil
1 large onion, chopped
½ cup (50 g) chopped celery
¼ cup (35 g) minced garlic
1 to 2 fresh hot peppers, seeded and minced
3 tablespoons chili powder
2 tablespoons cumin
3 tablespoons butter
½ cup (75 g) currants or raisins
½ cup (75 g) chopped carrots
1½ oz (45 g) bittersweet chocolate
Pinch of cinnamon

Cover the beans generously with water and soak overnight. Add more water if necessary. Bring to a boil and simmer until tender but not mushy, about 2 hours.

Put the chicken in a pot with 3 cups (750 ml) of water and the salt and pepper. Cover and simmer until the chicken is done, about 30 minutes. Remove the chicken from the broth and reserve the broth. Debone and skin the chicken and cut it into bite-size pieces.

Sauté the onion, celery, garlic, and hot pepper in the olive oil until tender. Add the chili powder, cumin, and butter, and sauté for 1 more minute.

Add the currants or raisins, carrots, 2 cups (500 ml) of the reserved chicken broth, chocolate, and cinnamon, along with the beans (drained of any excess cooking liquid). Add more broth if necessary. Let mixture cook, covered, on low heat about 45 minutes. Add the chicken, taste for seasoning, and simmer about 30 minutes longer. *Serves 8.*

Classic gumbo

Gumbo (an African word for okra) starts with a dark roux and is often thickened with okra and/or filé powder, made from the dried leaves of the sassafras tree. Serve with white rice.

For the roux:
½ cup (125 ml) canola oil
¾ cup (115 g) flour
1 quart (1 liter) chicken stock

For the gumbo:
2 lbs (1 kg) beef brisket (fat trimmed off) or 1 frying chicken, cut in large pieces
¼ cup (65 ml) canola oil
1 lb (500 g) fresh okra, finely sliced
2 large onions, chopped
1 bell pepper, chopped
1 cup (120 g) chopped celery
3 garlic cloves, minced
2 fresh hot peppers, seeded and minced
2 cups (400 g) peeled, seeded, and chopped tomatoes
2 bay leaves
1 tablespoon minced fresh thyme (or 1 teaspoon dried thyme)
1 to 2 lbs (500 g–1 kg) U.S. farmed or wild caught raw shrimp, shelled and deveined
About 2 lbs (1 kg) assorted seafood such as crab, fish, lobster, and crayfish (optional)
2 tablespoons filé powder
Salt and freshly ground pepper to taste

To make the roux: In a large heavy pot, combine the oil with the flour. Stirring constantly with a whisk or wooden spoon, cook over medium-high heat until the mixture turns a reddish brown, about 15 minutes. Bring the stock to a boil and add it slowly to the roux while constantly stirring. The mixture should thicken and become smooth.

To make the gumbo: In a large frying pan, brown the meat in the oil. Remove the meat and pour out and reserve the oil. Add 2 cups (500 ml) of water to the pan drippings and boil to dissolve. Scrape the drippings from the bottom of the pan and pour into a separate bowl.

Put the reserved oil back in the pan and add the okra, onions, bell pepper, celery, garlic, hot peppers, tomatoes, bay leaves, and thyme. Cook over low heat for about ½ hour until they are soft and slightly brown, then remove the vegetables from the pan and set aside. Return the meat to the pan, add the reserved drippings, cover, and simmer on low heat for 45 minutes or until tender.

To assemble the gumbo: Combine the roux mixture, the vegetables, and the stewed meat in one pot. Bring to a boil, add the shrimp and other seafood (if using), and cook about 5 minutes. Stir in the filé powder and let the gumbo rest 5 minutes to allow the filé to thicken before serving. Add salt and freshly ground pepper to taste. *Serves 6.*

Beerocks (stuffed bread pockets)

Many of our "heirloom" recipes came from English kitchens, but our early American heritage draws from other nationalities as well. This old family recipe from Jan Blüm's Grandma Bender originated in Germany. These days, Jan, owner of Seeds Blüm, uses a vegetarian filling instead of meat. As you may notice, beerocks are very similar to Russian piroshkis. Mustard is a good accompaniment.

For the dough:

2 cups (500 ml) whole milk
1/2 cup (215 g) sugar
1/2 cup (125 ml) vegetable oil
1 teaspoon salt
2 packages (14 g) dried yeast
6 cups (660 g) all-purpose flour

For the filling:

1/4 cup (65 ml) vegetable oil
1 lb (500 g) ground beef
2 large onions, chopped
1 large head cabbage, loosely shredded
A few leaves of kale or other leafy green (optional)
Salt and freshly ground black pepper

To make the dough: In a saucepan combine the milk, sugar, vegetable oil, and salt. Heat the mixture until the sugar has dissolved, but do not allow it to boil. Cool the mixture to lukewarm. Pour the milk mixture into the bowl of a heavy-duty mixer with a dough hook and stir the yeast into it. Add the flour 1 cup (110 g) at a time and knead with the dough hook until it forms a ball. Turn the dough over in an oiled bowl, cover with plastic wrap, and let it rise in a warm place such as a 200°F (95°C) oven until it doubles in size, about 2 hours. Punch the dough down and let it rise for another hour. While the dough is rising the second time, prepare the filling.

To make the filling: In a large frying pan, heat the oil and brown the meat and onions over medium heat. Add the cabbage (and other greens if desired) and salt and pepper to taste. Cover and cook until crisp-tender. The frying pan will be full at first, but the cabbage will shrink during cooking. Do not over-cook. Take off the cover as soon as the cabbage has wilted, or the mixture will become too "juicy."

Preheat the oven to 450°F (230°C) and grease a cookie sheet with some oil.

After the dough has risen, place it on a floured board. Roll it out as thin as possible into a rectangle. Cut it into 8-inch (20-cm) squares. Spoon 2 to 3 tablespoons of the filling into the center of each square, being careful not to get any oil on the dough edges. Join the four corners of each square in the center and pinch each seam closed to make an envelope. Place the beerocks on the oiled cookie sheet, then turn them seam side down to oil both sides. Bake them for about 15 to 20 minutes, until they are nicely browned. Serve immediately. *Serves 16 as a side dish, 8 as a main course.*

Baked beans with pork

A traditional recipe with a long history, baked beans are an American classic. In early America baked beans were not a vegetable dish but a pork dish; the beans were used to stretch the meat portion of the meal. The bean dish with molasses and salt pork we know today was first reported in 1840. This recipe is based on one from *The American Frugal Housewife* by Lydia Marie Child.

1 lb (500 g) red kidney or heirloom
   dry beans
1 tablespoon vegetable oil, or ¼ lb
   (125 g) salt pork, cut into 1-in
   (2.5-cm) cubes
1 lb (500 g) lean pork, fresh pork
   shoulder, or boneless pork chops,
   cut into 1-in- (2.5-cm-) wide strips
1 medium onion, chopped
⅓ teaspoon dried thyme
Freshly ground black pepper
¼ teaspoon salt

Pick over the beans, removing any debris, and wash them. Place them in a large saucepan and cover them with 2 inches (5 cm) of water. Either let them sit overnight or bring them to a boil for 1 minute, then remove from the heat and let them sit for 1 hour.

Cook the beans for 1 to 1½ hours until they are just tender. Drain them, setting the bean liquid aside.

In a large frying pan heat the oil (if using salt pork, sauté it for 2 or 3 minutes) and over fairly high heat brown half of the pork on all sides. Transfer it to a bean pot or a 3-quart (3-liter) covered Dutch oven. Repeat the process with the rest of the pork. Pour off the remaining grease. Carefully deglaze the pan with a little of the bean water and pour it over the pork. Add the beans, onion, thyme, pepper, and salt (omit the salt if you are using salt pork). Mix the ingredients and add enough bean liquid to just cover the beans. If you don't have enough liquid, add a little stock or boiling water. Cover the bean pot.

Bake at 300°F (150°C) for 4 to 6 hours. Check occasionally to make sure the liquid still covers the beans. If it gets too low, add more bean liquid or boiling water. Half an hour before the beans are done, uncover and let the beans brown slightly on top. *Serves 6 to 8.*

Bitter melon with beef stir-fry

Bitter flavors are an acquired taste, but if you enjoy bitter beer and radicchio you'll probably delight in this rich and complex dish. Serve it with steamed rice.

1 tablespoon dry sherry

1 tablespoon soy sauce

1 tablespoon cornstarch

½ lb (250 g) beef tenderloin, cut in thin strips across the grain

1 lb (500 g) bitter melon

½ teaspoon salt

1 red bell pepper

2 tablespoons peanut oil, divided

2 garlic cloves, minced

1 tablespoon grated fresh ginger root

2 tablespoons black bean sauce

2 teaspoons sugar

Garnish: 2 tablespoons of chopped fresh cilantro

Combine sherry, soy sauce, and cornstarch in a small bowl. Add the beef strips, coat thoroughly and set aside. Cut the bitter melon lengthwise; remove inside pulp and seeds. Slice thinly. Put into a bowl and sprinkle with salt. Let the melon sit for 20 minutes to remove some of the bitterness. After 20 minutes, squeeze out the water. Cut the red pepper in thin slices.

In a hot wok, heat 1 tablespoon of the oil. Add the bitter melon, garlic, and ginger and stir-fry for about 3 minutes. Remove the vegetables and put them on a warm serving plate. Add the remaining tablespoon of oil to the wok, heat and then add the beef strips. Stir over high heat until the meat starts to brown but is still pink inside. Add the marinating juices, bean sauce, 1 cup (250 ml) water, and the sugar. Cook for 1 more minute, but do not overcook. Arrange the beef strips over the vegetables on the platter. Garnish with chopped cilantro. *Serves 4.*

Pea shoots with crab sauce

Pea shoots are a special vegetable and greatly enjoyed in China. Here is an elegant pairing with crab. Serve this dish with steamed rice.

For the sauce:
2 garlic cloves, minced
1 tablespoon vegetable oil
1 tablespoon cornstarch
1 cup (250 ml) chicken stock
2 tablespoons sherry
½ lb (250 g) cooked Alaska king crab meat (about 1 cup)
4 tablespoons chopped, blanched Chinese leek leaves or 1 tablespoon chopped fresh Oriental chive leaves
Salt

For the pea shoots:
1 tablespoon sesame oil
1 quart (170 g) coarsely chopped fresh pea shoots

To make the sauce: In a saucepan over low heat, sauté the garlic in the vegetable oil until tender, about 1 minute. In a small bowl, blend the cornstarch with the chicken stock and sherry. Add the mixture to the pan and heat, stirring constantly until the sauce is thickened. Add the crabmeat and the Chinese leeks and simmer for another minute. Remove from the heat, and add salt to taste.

To make the pea shoots: In a wok or large pan, heat the sesame oil and stir-fry the pea shoots for about 3 minutes or until just tender. Lightly toss them with the sauce. *Serves 4.*

Shishito pepper and eggplant stir-fry with beef

I learned about cooking baby Japanese eggplants and using mioga ginger blossoms from a woman selling both at the local farmers' market. Serve this dish with a vegetable stir-fry and rice cooked with soybeans (see the recipe on page 150) for a complete meal.

For the marinade:
1 tablespoon dry sherry
2 tablespoons soy sauce
1 tablespoon cornstarch
¹⁄₂ teaspoon sugar
¹⁄₂ lb (250 g) beef filet strips

For the stir-fry:
2 tablespoons peanut oil
8 to 10 oz (250–300 g) Japanese baby eggplants, or larger eggplants cut into small strips
1 medium onion, chopped
16 green Shishito peppers or 1 sweet green Italian frying pepper cut into small strips
16 red Shishito peppers or 1 sweet red Italian frying pepper cut into small strips

6 mioga ginger blossoms, quartered (optional)
2 garlic cloves, minced
2 tablespoons fresh cilantro, chopped
2 teaspoons grated fresh ginger root
2 tablespoons oyster sauce
¹⁄₂ to ³⁄₄ cups (125–190 ml) chicken broth
¹⁄₂ teaspoon hot red pepper flakes

To make the marinade: In a small bowl, combine the sherry, soy sauce, cornstarch, and the sugar. Stir until the cornstarch is completely dissolved. Add the beef strips, toss, and set aside.

To make the stir-fry: Over high heat in a nonstick wok, heat the peanut oil until it is very hot. Add the eggplants and stir-fry over high heat for 3 minutes. Add the onion, green and red peppers, and ginger blossoms; stir-fry 2 more minutes. Toss in the minced garlic, cilantro, and grated ginger; cook for a couple of seconds. Put on a plate and set aside.

Heat the wok again, adding a little more peanut oil if necessary, and stir-fry the marinated beef for 1 minute or until medium rare. Return the vegetables to the wok, and then stir in the oyster sauce, the chicken broth, and the red pepper flakes. Heat together for another minute, and then serve the stir-fry at once over rice. *Serves 4.*

Grilled swordfish with rosemary

This recipe is from Carole Saville, author and herb maven. It blends the richness of swordfish with the assertiveness of rosemary. It works equally well when broiling the swordfish instead. Note that the swordfish needs to marinate for an hour. Many types of swordfish are threatened by overfishing. Look for domestic American swordfish, as it comes from well-managed sources.

¼ cup (10 g) fresh rosemary leaves and soft stems

1 cup (250 ml) olive oil

2 tablespoons lemon juice

¼ teaspoon salt

Cayenne pepper

4 yellowfin swordfish steaks, 1-in (2.5 cm) thick (about 5 oz/150 g each)

Garnish: 4 teaspoons finely chopped fresh rosemary, rosemary flowers (if in bloom), and lemon wedges

Finely chop the rosemary. Put it in a small bowl and with the bottom of a drinking glass rub the rosemary to bruise it. In a large, deep plate, combine the olive oil, lemon juice, salt, cayenne pepper, and rosemary, stirring to combine. Rinse the swordfish and pat it dry. Turn each steak over in the marinade to coat it well. Cover and refrigerate the swordfish for 1 hour, turning it once after 30 minutes.

Grill the swordfish over a medium flame, turning it after 5 minutes. Continue to grill until the flesh is opaque when cut in the thickest part, about 5 more minutes. Remove the steaks and place on four warmed plates. Sprinkle 1 teaspoon of chopped rosemary over each serving. Further garnish with rosemary flowers and lemon wedges. Serve immediately. *Serves 4.*

Stir-fried shrimp and greens

David Cunningham, one-time staff horticulturist at the Vermont Bean Seed Company, created this recipe to take advantage of his many Asian greens. When possible look for trap-caught, U.S. farmed, or trawl-caught shrimp. Serve this stir-fry with steamed rice.

For the shrimp marinade:
1 tablespoon tomato paste
1 tablespoon cornstarch
1 tablespoon soy sauce
2 tablespoons vinegar
2 tablespoons water
½ teaspoon Chinese mustard
1½ lbs (725 g) raw shrimp, shelled, cleaned, and deveined

For the sauce:
½ cup (125 ml) chicken stock
1 tablespoon cornstarch
1 tablespoon soy sauce
2 teaspoons honey
4 large garlic cloves, minced

For the stir-fry:
¼ cup (65 ml) peanut oil, divided
2 large heads pac choi, stems sliced diagonally in 2-in (5-cm) pieces
4 scallions (green onions), sliced diagonally
1 quart (280 g) tatsoi leaves

To make the marinade: Mix the marinade ingredients together, add the shrimp, and refrigerate for 3 hours. Drain and reserve both the liquid and the shrimp.

To make the sauce: Mix the sauce ingredients together, add the drained marinade liquid and set aside.

To make the stir-fry: Heat the wok over high heat and add about half the oil. Stir-fry the shrimp quickly in small batches. As they are cooked, put the shrimp and any juices into a bowl and reserve.

Add the remaining oil and stir-fry the pac choi stems and scallions for about 1 minute. Add the tatsoi leaves and stir until they are wilted. Add the sauce, lower the heat, and stir until thickened. Add the cooked shrimp together with their liquid. Heat all together while stirring, for 1 more minute. *Serves 6 to 8.*

Steamed rice

Steamed white rice is basic to all of Asia. In China and Japan they use short-grain rice. In India, however, they commonly use a long-grain, or fragrant basmati rice. The following recipe is the most basic and applicable to most white rice varieties. If you use a rice cooker, follow the proportions and directions that come with it. An interesting variation, and one packed with nutrition, is to make the rice with fresh green soybeans. The beans will cook in the same amount of time as the rice.

1½ cups (340 g) uncooked white rice
2 cups (800 ml) water
Optional: 1 cup (200 g) shelled green soybeans

Rinse the rice under running water, then drain and place in a pot with a tight-fitting lid. (If using, add the optional green soybeans to the rice at this point.) Cover and bring to a boil. Reduce the heat to low and simmer for 15 minutes. Turn off the heat (don't lift the lid!) and let it sit covered for another 15 minutes. Fluff lightly and then serve. *Serves 4.*

Golden chicken curry with garam masala

I learned to make "real" curry from my friend Bhadra Fancy, who grew up outside Bombay. What a difference! Instead of a generic mix of spices in a tin, you grind your own fresh aromatic spices, including your own hot peppers. Called garam masala in India, the spices in curry vary from region to region, cook to cook, and from season to season.

A vegetarian version is quite wonderful as well. Here, instead of chicken, whole baby eggplants, potatoes, a whole cauliflower cut in florets, and snap beans are simmered with the garam masala. These curries are served over rice with raita (a yogurt and mint sauce) and flat breads.

For the masala paste:

- 1 tablespoon whole coriander seeds
- 1 tablespoon whole cumin seeds
- ½ teaspoon cardamom seeds (the seeds from about 6 pods)
- 10 black peppercorns
- 1 teaspoon ground cinnamon
- ¼ teaspoon ground cloves
- 2 teaspoons ground turmeric
- 1 teaspoon ground cayenne pepper
- 2 teaspoons salt
- 2 tablespoons poppy seeds
- 12 whole blanched almonds
- 5 tablespoons unsweetened coconut milk
- 1 cup (100 g) chopped onions
- 8 garlic cloves
- ½-in (3-mm) piece fresh ginger, peeled and sliced
- 1 or 2 yellow or red fresh jalapeño peppers, seeded
- 1 yellow or red fresh cayenne pepper, seeded

For the curry:

- 2 tablespoons vegetable oil
- 1 (3-lb/1.5-kg) chicken, skin removed, cut into serving pieces
- 1 onion, chopped
- 2 yellow bell peppers, cut in ½-in (13-mm) pieces
- 8 Italian paste tomatoes, peeled, seeded, and chopped
- 2 cups (300 g) whole baby carrots, or large carrots cut in thick coins
- 8 small potatoes, peeled
- 1 tablespoon lemon juice

To make the masala paste: In a dry frying pan, toast the coriander, cumin, and cardamom seeds over medium heat until they just begin to perfume the air. Cool and then combine the toasted seeds and the peppercorns and grind them into a powder using a spice grinder or a mortar and pestle. In a food processor or blender, blend the toasted ground spices and the remaining ingredients into a smooth paste. Set the masala paste aside.

To make the curry: In a Dutch oven, heat the vegetable oil. Add the chicken pieces and brown them over medium heat for about 20 minutes or until they are a rich golden brown. Remove the chicken from the pan.

Add the onion and bell peppers to the same pan and sauté over medium heat until they are soft, about 5 minutes. Add the chopped tomatoes, the reserved masala paste, and 4 cups (1 liter) of water. Stir and bring the mixture to a simmer. Return the chicken pieces to the pan, add the carrots and potatoes, and simmer covered for about 30 minutes. Stir in the lemon juice. Serve the curry with rice. *Serves 6.*

New england boiled dinner

A boiled dinner has long been a favorite coldwinter-night dish. A particular favorite in colonial America, it could have been boiled up over the fire a good part of the day, needing little attention. Further, leftovers could be cooked up in hash the next day. Avoid the plastic-wrapped brisket from the supermarket, as it is tough and fatty. Get a lean one from a butcher. Serve with mustard, horseradish, and/or pickles.

3 to 4 lbs (1.5–2 kg) extra-lean corned beef brisket

2 tablespoons pickling spice in a cheesecloth bag, or 6 whole cloves, 4 whole allspice, ½ teaspoon peppercorns, 1 tablespoon mustard seeds, and 2 bay leaves in cheesecloth bag

5 or 6 medium potatoes, quartered

5 or 6 medium carrots, cut into chunks

2 large onions, thickly sliced

4 turnips and/or 4 golden beets, peeled and quartered (optional)

1 medium head cabbage, cut into 6 or 8 wedges

For the glaze:

⅓ cup (85 ml) Dijon mustard

¼ teaspoon ground cloves

2 tablespoons brown sugar

In a large kettle or Dutch oven, cover the meat with water. Boil for half an hour; pour off the water and discard it. Add fresh boiling water to cover the meat, add spices, and simmer for 45 minutes per pound of meat (minus the first half hour), or until fork-tender. Remove the meat to an ovenproof pan, fat-side up. Add the potatoes, carrots, and onions (and turnips and beets, if desired) to the kettle, cover, and boil for 15 minutes. Place the cabbage on top of the other vegetables and cook 10 more minutes, or until tender. Preheat the oven to 350°F (175°C).

Meanwhile, glaze the beef. Paint the mustard on the beef, sprinkle with cloves, then with the brown sugar. Bake for 15 to 20 minutes. Place the meat on a large serving platter and surround it with the vegetables. (Discard cooking water and spices.) Cut the meat across the grain. *Serves 6 to 8.*

Pickled mustard cabbage stir-fry with pork

Mai Truong, who grew up in Vietnam, shared with me her favorite dish using pickled mustard—in this case with pork. I've also enjoyed adding shredded bamboo shoots, pea pods, and carrots to this recipe. Serve this dish with rice and soy sauce. For a complete meal accompany it with another stir-fry and a light soup. If you can't make your own, pickled mustard is available in the refrigerated section of most Asian markets.

½ lb (250 g) lean pork, cut in thin
   strips across the grain
⅛ teaspoon salt
6 garlic cloves, minced, divided
1 lb (500 g) pickled mustard cabbage
   (see recipe on page 31)
2 tablespoons vegetable oil
Fresh cilantro leaves, chopped
Fresh scallions (green onions),
   chopped

Sprinkle the pork strips with the salt and half the minced garlic. Marinate the mixture for about 1 hour. Drain the pickled mustard and chop it into 1-inch (2.5-cm) pieces. In a hot wok heat the oil. Sauté the remaining garlic until it is starting to turn golden. Add the pork strips and stir-fry until the meat turns gray. Add the pickled mustard and ½ cup (125 ml) of water. Cook for 3 more minutes, transfer to a warm platter and garnish the dish with cilantro and scallions. *Serves 4.*

Babyback ribs with ancho chilies

All types of flavorings, including ground dried cayenne, paprika-types, and mirasol/guajillo chilies as well as ancho chilies, can be used in a dry rub to flavor ribs. Other traditional flavorings include ground oregano and cumin, brown sugar, dry mustard, and garlic. You can create your own formula using your favorite dried hot pepper or try the one given here.

Accompany the ribs with your favorite barbecue sauce, mashed potatoes, and coleslaw or a salad.

4 tablespoons ground dried ancho
    chilies
2 teaspoons salt
$1/4$ teaspoon ground cumin
1 teaspoon brown sugar
4 to 6 lbs (2–3 kg) babyback (loin)
    pork ribs

Blend the ground chilies, salt, cumin, and sugar in a small bowl. Rub the ribs with the mixture, thoroughly covering both sides. Cover the ribs tightly with plastic wrap and refrigerate for 6 to 8 hours or overnight.

Preheat the oven to 300°F (150°C). Wrap the ribs in aluminum foil and bake for 1 hour or until tender. Remove from the oven, unwrap, cool, and reserve.

Barbecue the ribs on a gas grill over fairly high heat for about 10 to 15 minutes. Turn them a few times to make sure they cook evenly. *Serves 4.*

Roast pork with fennel stuffing

This pork recipe is "home cooking" at its best. My favorite way to serve it is with puréed celeriac or mashed potatoes, gravy made from the pan juices, and fresh peas. My family really loves stuffing, so sometimes I double the stuffing amount and bake it separately in a covered casserole at 350°F (175°C) for about 45 minutes.

Boned and rolled pork loin (approxi-
    mately 3 lbs/1.5 kg)
Freshly ground black pepper

For the stuffing:
1 medium Florence fennel bulb
2 tablespoons butter
1 medium onion, chopped
4 cups (360 g) dry bread cubes
2 Fuji, Granny Smith, or Braeburn
    apples, peeled and cut into $1/3$-in
    (3-cm) dice
1 teaspoon ground sage or poultry
    seasoning
$1/3$ teaspoon celery seeds
$1/3$ cup (85 ml) chicken broth
Salt and freshly ground black pepper
1 egg

Preheat the oven to 350°F (175°C).

Untie the pork loin and unfold it. Season the outside of the roast with pepper. Refrigerate the meat until it's time to roast it.

To make the stuffing: Wash the fennel bulb, cut off the stem and its greens. Cut the bulb in half lengthwise, put it facedown on a cutting board, and chop it into $1/4$-inch (6-mm) pieces.

In a medium frying pan heat the butter over medium heat. Add the fennel and onion and sauté for about 10 minutes, or until they're translucent. Stir occasionally to keep the vegetables from sticking. In a large bowl combine the bread cubes, onion mixture, and apples. Sprinkle on the sage and celery seeds and pour in the chicken broth. Mix and season to taste. Add the egg and mix thoroughly.

To stuff the pork: Lay out the pork loin and spread the stuffing mixture on one half. (Put any leftover stuffing in a small ovenproof dish, cover, and bake for about 45 minutes.) Pull the other half of the pork loin over the stuffing. Tie four or five pieces of string around the loin to replace the ones that you cut off. Tie a piece around the ends too.

Place the stuffed pork on a rack in a small roasting pan. Roast for a little more than 2 hours or until a meat thermometer registers 175 to 180°F (79–82°C). Let the roast sit for 10 minutes or so before serving. Remove the strings and cut the roast into 1-inch- (2.5-cm-) wide slices. *Serves 6.*

Flavorful sides

Chayote sauté with chilies

Chayotes are delicate-tasting, slightly sweet squashlike vegetables. They can be simply sautéed in a little oil and enjoyed as is or sauced with tomatoes and sprinkled with cheese or minced chilies of any measure of hotness to create a spicy side dish like the following. Serve this dish to accompany egg, cheese, fish, and chicken dishes or add it to tacos or burritos.

1½ lbs (725 g) chayote (about 3 large)
2 teaspoons vegetable oil
2 cloves garlic, thinly sliced
Minced chilies to taste: ½ tablespoon jalapeño for mild, ½ tablespoon serrano for medium, or 1 teaspoon, or more, habañero for blazing
½ teaspoon crumbled dried Mexican oregano leaves
¼ teaspoon salt
2 tablespoons water
Garnish: 1 tablespoon fresh chopped cilantro

Peel the chayote and cut it into slices ¼ inch (13 mm) thick, including the seed, which is edible. Pour oil into a medium sauté pan, heat over fairly low heat, and add the chayote. Sauté for about 10 minutes or until the chayote starts to brown slightly, stirring occasionally so it cooks evenly and doesn't get too brown. Add the garlic and sauté lightly. Add the chilies, oregano, salt, and water, stir, and cover; simmer until the chayote is tender and translucent, about 5 minutes. Transfer to a warm serving dish and garnish with cilantro. *Serves 4.*

Grandma Alice's summer vegetables

This recipe was given to me by Renee Shepherd of Renee's Garden seed company. Renee's Grandma Alice made this dish for her when she was a kid after she let her pick all the vegetables. Renee loved all the colors. Here, the onions and carrots add sweetness while the fresh squash tastes quite nutty and creamy.

When I tried it I used small squash cut in pieces, as Renee recommends. Subsequently, I have also made it using only the tiniest baby squashes, such as pattypans, crooknecks, and zucchini, along with baby carrots. In that case, the squash and carrots should be left whole to really enjoy their beauty.

4 to 5 cups (700–875 g) green and
    gold summer squashes, cut into
    1-in (2.5-cm) pieces (4 to 5
    medium squashes)
2 medium carrots, sliced
1 large onion, coarsely chopped
1 cup (250 ml) rich chicken stock
2 tablespoons butter
2¹/₂ tablespoons chopped fresh dill
1 tablespoon chopped fresh Italian
    parsley
Salt and freshly ground black pepper
2 tablespoons freshly grated Parme-
    san or Asiago cheese

In a 3-quart (3-liter) Dutch oven, combine the vegetables with the chicken broth and the butter. Bring the mixture to a boil and then reduce the heat and simmer for about 8 to 10 minutes or until the carrots and squash are just tender.

Remove the pan from the heat and mix in the dill, parsley, salt and pepper. Serve immediately with the freshly grated Parmesan or Asiago cheese. *Serves 6.*

Succotash

Many Native American tribes combined beans with corn, thereby forming a complete protein. Succotash is one such combination dish, and it was made with fresh corn and shelled beans in midsummer and from reconstituted dried sweet corn and beans during the rest of the year. Here is my favorite recipe, made with fresh limas and corn. The variation with bacon would be a typical Southern version. See page 83 for tips on removing corn kernels from the cob.

3 tablespoons salted butter
½ onion, chopped
Fresh hot pepper to taste, minced (optional)
½ sweet pepper (green, red, or yellow)
2 cups (400 g) fresh corn kernels (approximately 4 ears)
2 cups (approximately 1 lb/500 g) fresh shelled lima beans
Salt and freshly ground black pepper
⅓ cup (85 ml) milk or light cream (optional)

In a saucepan, melt the butter and sauté the onion (and hot pepper if desired) a few minutes to soften it. Add the sweet pepper and cook a few more minutes. Add the corn, beans, and 1 cup (250 ml) of water; cover; and simmer for about 15 minutes or until the limas are tender (large limas take longer). Add salt and pepper to taste (and add milk if desired) and serve. *Serves 4.*

Variation: Instead of using butter, cook 2 strips of bacon in a separate frying pan until crisp. Remove the bacon and set it aside. Sauté the onion and pepper in the bacon fat. Put the sautéed onion and pepper in a saucepan with the corn, beans, and water and cook as above. Garnish with crumbled bits of the reserved bacon. *Serves 4.*

Braised belgian endive

Belgian endive is an elegant, slightly bitter vegetable that has long been associated with French cooking. It's best with a long braising to make it luscious and to sweeten and mellow the bitterness. Belgian endive is a classic accompaniment to beef and lamb.

6 large (6-oz/200-g) Belgian endives
2 tablespoons butter
1 tablespoon fresh lemon juice
Salt and freshly ground black pepper

Trim the base of the endives, wash them well, and drain. Melt the butter over low heat in a heavy sauté pan and add the endives. Add ¾ cup (190 ml) water and the lemon juice, bring to a boil, and add salt and pepper to taste. Lower heat and cover the pan with a round sheet of buttered parchment paper and a lid. Simmer for about 45 minutes, until the endives are tender, occasionally turning and basting them with the liquid, which will begin to reduce. Turn up the heat and reduce the remaining liquid. Once the liquid has evaporated, let the endives brown slightly, turning them once or twice. Serve immediately, or refrigerate and reheat when needed. *Serves 6.*

Tarragon and balsamic vinegar—braised onions

In Italy, all sorts of onions are popular, especially when baked. The addition of balsamic vinegar and tarragon is a bonus. Roasted with just a little olive oil, onions are low in fat and calories and are the perfect appetizer or side dish for a holiday roast.

6 medium red onions, peeled
4 tablespoons extra-virgin olive oil
5 tablespoons balsamic vinegar
1 tablespoon fresh chopped tarragon
Dash of salt
Freshly ground black pepper

Preheat the oven to 350°F (175°C). Place the onions in a baking dish, sprinkle them with olive oil, vinegar, tarragon, salt, and pepper. Bake for about 1 1/2 to 2 hours, or until they're tender and lightly browned. Baste them often with the liquid as they bake. *Serves 6.*

Fava beans with tomatoes

Fava beans are enjoyed in Mexico and this is one of the most popular ways to serve them. The same recipe can be used for snap beans as well. Just add cooked beans to the sauce and simmer for 2 or 3 minutes.

**4 to 5 lbs (2–2.5 kg) fresh fava
beans, shelled (about 4 cups)**

For the sauce:
1 white onion
2 cloves garlic, unpeeled
4 paste tomatoes
1 teaspoon lard
½ teaspoon dried Mexican oregano
1 teaspoon salt

To prepare the beans: Remove the fava beans from their pods. Boil them in water for 5 minutes. Drain and cool. Remove the tough skins by cutting a small slit at one end of the bean and, with your index finger and thumb, squeezing the bean from its skin.

To make the sauce: Peel the onion and cut it into 8 wedges. Heat a comal or cast-iron pan and toast the onion wedges until golden brown and the unpeeled garlic until soft, about 10 minutes. Cool and peel the garlic. Toast the tomatoes until their skins start to blister. Cool them, peel, and remove the seeds. Place the toasted onion, garlic, and tomatoes into a blender and purée until smooth. In a saucepan, heat the lard and fry the tomato purée—be careful, it splatters—for about 3 minutes. Add 1½ cups (375 ml) water, Mexican oregano, and salt.

Add the fava beans (or cooked snap beans) to the sauce; simmer for 5 to 10 minutes or until the beans are soft but don't fall apart. *Serves 4.*

Carrots with chervil butter

Chervil is a delicate-tasting herb that complements carrots well. If none is available, substitute a lesser amount of tarragon.

1 to 2 tablespoons unsalted butter, at room temperature

4 to 5 teaspoons finely chopped fresh chervil, or 2 teaspoons fresh tarragon

1 lb (500 g) small varieties of carrots or large carrots cut in 1½-in (4-cm) diagonal slices

Pinch of salt

Garnish: sprigs of chervil

To make the butter: Cut the butter into a few pieces and mash it with a fork to soften. Then slowly incorporate the chervil. Use a rubber spatula to put the mixture into a small container and set aside.

To make the carrots: Lightly peel the carrots but leave a small piece of the stem and root end. Bring a large pot of water to a boil. Add the carrots and boil for about 5 minutes, or until they're just tender. Drain. Put the herb butter in a sauté pan and warm over low heat. Just as the butter starts to melt, add the carrots and salt and toss to coat them with the butter. Transfer the carrots to a warm serving dish. Garnish with sprigs of chervil and serve. *Serves 4.*

Braised red cabbage

This dish is most often associated with northern France and Germany. The brilliant red color is achieved by adding acidic vinegar and red wine to the cabbage. Serve this cabbage dish with roast chicken or pork and mashed potatoes.

2 tablespoons butter
1 onion, thinly sliced
1 medium red cabbage, shredded (about 8 cups/560 g)
1 tart apple, peeled, cored, and sliced
1 tablespoon sugar
1 tablespoon red wine vinegar
½ cup (125 ml) good red wine
1 bay leaf
Salt and freshly ground black pepper

Melt the butter in a Dutch oven or a soup pot. Add the onions and sauté them over medium heat until they are soft, about 7 minutes. Add the cabbage, apple, sugar, vinegar, red wine, and the bay leaf. Stir the ingredients together and simmer on low for 30 to 40 minutes, or until the cabbage is tender. Remove the bay leaf and season with salt and pepper. *Serves 6.*

Corn pudding

I modified this recipe after hearing the dish described by Debra Friedman at Old Sturbridge Village, a New England living history museum. She called it by its colonial name, green corn pudding. The sweet corn kernels enveloped in rich custard is as big a treat today as it must have been years ago. See page 83 for tips on removing corn kernels from the cob. Serve the pudding as a side dish with meat and poultry or as a hearty lunch with a salad.

1 tablespoon salted butter
1 medium onion, finely chopped
3 cups (650 g) fresh sweet corn kernels (7–8 plump ears)
2 cups (500 ml) whole milk
6 large eggs, slightly beaten
Dash of freshly grated nutmeg
1 teaspoon sugar (optional)

Preheat the oven to 350°F (175°C).

In a small nonstick pan, melt the butter over medium heat. Sauté the onion until translucent, about 7 minutes. In a large bowl add the onion, corn, milk, eggs, and nutmeg (and sugar if the corn is not very sweet), and mix well. Pour the mixture into a small casserole or a 9-inch (23-cm) pottery pie dish. Bake for 1 hour, or until lightly brown and a knife inserted halfway into the center comes out clean. *Serves 6 as a side dish.*

Savory mashed potatoes with garden herbs

Traditional mashed potatoes are wonderful, but adding chopped fresh herbs means infinite variations.

2 to 2½ lbs (1–1.2 kg) Yukon Gold or Russet-type potatoes (approximately 4 large potatoes), peeled and cut into quarters
2 garlic cloves
½ cup (125 ml) milk
⅓ cup (85 ml) heavy cream
4 tablespoons butter
1½ teaspoons finely snipped fresh chives
1 tablespoon finely chopped fresh parsley
1½ teaspoons finely chopped fresh tarragon
Dash of nutmeg
Salt and freshly ground black pepper

In a large saucepan, cover the potatoes and garlic with water and boil for 10 to 15 minutes, or until the potatoes are tender. Be careful not to overcook them. Drain off the water.

Meanwhile, in a small saucepan, heat the milk and cream. When the mixture is hot but not boiling, add the butter and continue heating until the butter has melted.

Force the potatoes and garlic through a ricer or foodmill, or mash them in a bowl with a potato masher until they are smooth. (Be careful not to overmix them, or the potatoes will get gummy.) Place the potatoes in a large saucepan and over medium heat, slowly stir in the milk mixture with a spoon until it has a creamy texture. Fold in the herbs. Add salt and pepper to taste. *Serves 4.*

Brussels sprouts with cream and nuts

Brussels sprouts were one of the many vegetables that Thomas Jefferson introduced to America, and they quickly became popular. Be careful not to overcook them. They are wonderful combined with any kind of nuts.

½ to 1 cup (50–100 g) walnuts, hazelnuts, or roasted and peeled chestnuts (about 2–3 oz)

1½ lbs (about 6 cups/725 g) Brussels sprouts

2 tablespoons salted butter

¾ cup (190 ml) heavy cream (or substitute light cream)

Salt and freshly ground black pepper

Freshly ground nutmeg to taste

If using walnuts or hazelnuts, first roast them at 300°F (150°C) until fragrant but not brown, about 10 minutes. Rub the skins off the hazelnuts. Chop the nuts coarsely and set aside.

Wash the Brussels sprouts thoroughly and cut a small X in the bottom of each one to ensure even cooking. Bring about 3 cups (750 ml) of water to a boil, add the sprouts, and cook for 5 to 10 minutes, until barely tender. Drain the Brussels sprouts. In a medium frying pan, melt the butter and sauté the Brussels sprouts over low heat for about 3 minutes. Add the cream and nuts; season to taste with salt, pepper, and nutmeg; and simmer, stirring, for 3 minutes. *Serves 6.*

Carrot and garlic stir-fry

This popular vegetable stir-fry contrasts sweet and hot. Its richness combines well with other dishes containing the cool flavors of pac choi, cabbage, or spinach.

1½ tablespoons vegetable oil

1 lb (500 g) carrots, peeled and cut into coins (about 3 cups)

2 large garlic cloves, peeled and minced

2 scallions (green onions), sliced thinly

¼ teaspoon hot red pepper flakes

¼ teaspoon salt

1 to 2 tablespoons chopped fresh cilantro leaves

Garnish: cilantro leaves

Pour the oil into a wok. Heat over high heat until very hot. Add the carrots and stir-fry for 3 or 4 minutes, add the garlic and scallions and stir to mix. Continue to stir-fry until the carrots are tender but still slightly crunchy. Add the red pepper, salt, and cilantro and mix. Taste and adjust the seasonings if necessary. To serve, pour contents of wok onto a small platter and garnish with cilantro leaves. Serve at once. *Serves 3 to 4 as a side dish.*

Italian-style beans

Preparing beans in the Italian manner means cooking them twice. Bring a large pot of water to a boil, add the beans—be they green or yellow snap beans, romano beans, shelled horticultural beans, or fresh favas—to the water and cook them until they are just tender but still have a hint of crunch. Drain them and then reheat them with flavorings before serving. Butter is sometimes used in this last stage, but a more common finish for the beans is to reheat them in olive oil and garlic and then sprinkle them with Parmigiano-Reggiano cheese. Sometimes mashed anchovies are added to the olive oil.

Following are two variations on Italian beans.

1 lb (500 g) shelled fresh fava beans
  (2 to 2½ lbs/1–1.2 kgs of large
  fava bean pods)
1½ tablespoons extra-virgin olive oil
2 garlic cloves, minced
Salt and freshly ground black pepper
Freshly grated Parmigiano-Reggiano
  cheese

Variation:
1 lb (500 g) green or yellow
  'Romano' or snap beans
1½ tablespoons olive oil
2 garlic cloves, minced
Salt and freshly ground black pepper
Freshly grated Parmigiano-Reggiano
  cheese

In a large saucepan, bring 6 to 8 cups (1.5–2 liters) of water to a boil. Add the shelled fava beans and cook them until tender, about 8 to 12 minutes depending on their size. Pour the beans into a colander and let them cool for a few minutes. If the beans are fairly mature, the outside skin must be removed at this time. Very young beans, ½ inch (4 cm) or so in diameter, need no peeling.

In a small frying pan, heat the oil and sauté the garlic for a few minutes, but do not let it brown. Add the peeled favas and bring them to serving temperature. Lightly salt and pepper the beans. Adjust seasonings, transfer them to a warm bowl, and sprinkle on cheese. *Serves 4.*

Variation: Wash and string the beans if necessary. Remove the stem ends. If the beans are large, cut them into 2-inch (5-cm) lengths. Precook the beans as described above. They will cook from 4 to 7 minutes, depending on their size and age. ('Romano' beans cook more quickly than standard snap beans.) Cook until they are just tender. Drain the beans and proceed as described above. *Serves 4.*

Grilled red and gold peppers with melted anchovies, garlic, and basil sauce

This is a favorite recipe of Renee Shepherd, founder of Renee's Garden seed company. Once I made it I had to agree. She developed it when working with her cooking partner Fran Raboff. Accompany the peppers with slices of crusty bread.

2 large sweet peppers, one red and
  one yellow
1 tablespoon extra-virgin olive oil
1 two-oz (65-g) can anchovies,
  drained and coarsely chopped
6 garlic cloves, minced
2 tablespoons balsamic vinegar
½ cup (15 g) chopped fresh Italian
  parsley
½ cup (25 g) chopped fresh basil

Preheat a charcoal or gas grill. Remove the seeds and membranes from the peppers and cut them lengthwise into 1-inch- (2.5-cm-) wide strips. Brush them with olive oil and grill them until they are slightly charred and tender, from 5 to 7 minutes. Set the peppers aside.

In a heavy frying pan, heat 1 tablespoon of olive oil. Add the chopped anchovies and the garlic and cook over low to medium heat, stirring, until the anchovies melt and the garlic is fragrant, about 2 to 3 minutes. Stir in the balsamic vinegar. Add the parsley and basil and remove from the heat.

Arrange the grilled pepper strips on a serving platter and spoon the sauce over them. Serve immediately. *Serves 4.*

Haricots verts

France's most famous kind of bean is the *haricot vert*, a thin filet-type string bean. To quote Escoffier, considered the father of modern French cooking, "Haricots verts are one of the finest vegetables one can serve." French chefs I've spoken with refer to them reverently and use them to garnish a plate only when they think a dish is special. Traditionally haricots verts are served with only butter and salt and pepper. With such a naked presentation, quality is critical.

1 lb (4 cups/500 g) tiny filet beans haricots verts
1 tablespoon butter
Salt and freshly ground black pepper
Garnish: finely chopped fresh parsley

Trim the beans. Bring a large pot of water to a boil. Add the beans and cook them for 4 to 6 minutes, uncovered, until they're tender but still slightly firm. Drain. Add the butter in small pieces and toss. Season with salt and pepper to taste. Sprinkle lightly with parsley. *Serves 4.*

Braised lettuce with lemon thyme

Few folks think of cooking lettuce, but it actually makes a velvety vegetable with a delicate taste. I learned to fold the lettuce heads into packets from Jacques Pepin's book *La Technique*; this braised lettuce makes a dramatic presentation at a dinner party. Traditionally this dish is served with carrots or peas and accompanies beef, lamb, or fish.

2 large butterhead lettuces, Bibb or Boston types
Salt and freshly ground black pepper
2 tablespoons melted butter, divided
1 teaspoon lemon juice
1 tablespoon finely chopped fresh lemon thyme
Garnish: Lemon thyme

Bring a large pot of salted water to a boil. Wash and clean the lettuce heads of any grit. Drop the lettuce into the boiling water. Place a wet paper towel on top of the lettuce to keep it under the water. Boil the lettuce uncovered for about 5 minutes, until the core feels tender when pierced with a knife. Carefully remove the lettuce. Place it under cold running water to cool. Squeeze out excess water, retaining the natural form of the lettuce. Place the lettuce on a cutting board and cut it in half. Cut especially large heads into quarters. Place the piece cut-side down on a cutting board and fold the leafy green part up onto the center of the lettuce. Now fold the core end over it. Trim most of the core off so it will fold fairly flat. You should now have little triangular packets. Sprinkle lightly with salt and pepper. Set them aside.

In a small bowl, blend 1 tablespoon of the melted butter, the lemon juice, and the chopped lemon thyme. Spread the mixture on the top side of the lettuce packets. In a large nonstick frying pan, heat the remaining butter. Place the lettuce packets into the frying pan, folded-side up. Sprinkle with salt and pepper. Cook over medium heat for about 5 minutes, until they're lightly browned. Turn them gently, season with salt and pepper, and cook about 4 minutes on the other side. Arrange them on a serving platter, folded-side down. Garnish with sprigs of lemon thyme. *Serves 2.*

79

E FAMILY

Butter Sauce flavored with Lemon

flavored with lemon juice,
k, yellow, creamy   the most
easy

Asparagus with hollandaise sauce

Perfectly cooked, fresh-picked asparagus is the gardener's reward for care and patience. For a special occasion, gild this lily-family vegetable with a rich hollandaise sauce.

The velvety texture and richness of hollandaise is the result of the artful combination of egg yolks and melted butter.

The trick to making hollandaise is to allow the egg yolks to slowly absorb the butter and seasonings and not allow them to curdle. You must not let the mixture get too hot (or you will scramble the egg yolks), nor add the melted butter too quickly (or it will separate).

Hollandaise can be made by hand with a wire whisk or in a blender or food processor. The first few times you make it, I recommend doing it by hand so that you have more control. If you want to use a blender or food processor, check the manufacturer's guide for your machine.

For the sauce:

6 to 8 tablespoons butter

3 egg yolks

1 to 2 tablespoons fresh lemon juice

Salt and freshly ground black pepper

For the asparagus:

2 to 3 lbs (1–1.5 kg) asparagus

Salt

To make the sauce: Melt the butter in a saucepan. Keep it warm but not boiling. Put the egg yolks and 1 tablespoon water in the top of a double boiler and whisk them together for 30 seconds or until they start to thicken. Place the pan over water simmering in the bottom of the double boiler and whisk the mixture until the eggs thicken enough for you to see the bottom of the pan between strokes, approximately 2 minutes. (Do not let the water in the bottom of the double boiler boil or touch the bottom of the top pan.) Have a bowl of cold water nearby in case the eggs start to curdle, so you can quickly submerge the bottom of the pan to cool it.

Once the eggs have thickened, remove the double boiler from the heat. Beat the sauce well and start adding the warm butter, a few dribbles at a time, while continuing to beat the mixture. The process takes 3 to 4 minutes. As the sauce thickens, you can add the butter more rapidly. Do not include the butter's milky residue in the sauce. When all the butter has been absorbed, add the lemon juice and salt and pepper to taste. Keep the sauce warm over hot, not boiling, water while you prepare the asparagus.

To prepare the asparagus: Take each spear and snap off the lower end at the point where it breaks readily. Use the tough ends for soup or discard them. Wash the spears well to remove grit.

Select a large oval roasting pan or deep casserole and fill it three quarters full with water. For each quart (liter) of water add 1 teaspoon salt. Bring the water to a boil. Add the asparagus and boil until done, about 3 to 6 minutes. Pierce a stalk with a fork to test for doneness. Well-cooked asparagus is slightly tender, a bit crunchy, and bright green. Remove the asparagus from the pan with tongs and drain well on a towel. Serve immediately, as is or with hollandaise sauce.

To serve, pour the sauce into a small pitcher or spoon a few tablespoons over asparagus spears. *Serves 6.*

Baked winter squash with maple nut/seed butter

A wonderful complement to squash is a nut or seed butter. The rich flavors seem meant for each other. You can make your own nut or seed butter, and many types are available in natural food and specialty stores. Only basic baking directions are given below; cooking times and the number of people served depend on the size and variety of squash.

2 acorn or other small squash (about 1¼ lb/625 g each), or 1 medium squash (about 2½ lb/1.2 kg)
3 tablespoons salted butter
3 tablespoons nut or seed butter
3 tablespoons maple syrup

Preheat the oven to 350°F (175°C). Place the squash on a baking pan and cook for ¾ to 1½ hours, until soft. You may want to turn the squash a couple of times for more even cooking. Cut the squash in half and remove the seeds (wash and save them to toast for snacks) and strings; if using one squash, cut the pieces again to make four servings. Return the squash to the baking pan, cut-sides up. In a small saucepan, melt the butter, add nut or seed butter and syrup, and stir to mix. Spoon the butter mixture into the squash cavities and coat the surface of the squash. Return the squash to the oven for about 10 minutes to heat it through before serving. *Serves 4 as a side dish.*

Show-off barbecued vegetables

One of the tastiest and showiest ways of preparing summer vegetables is a quick and easy adaptation of the ever-popular barbecue. Although meat, fish, or poultry can be a nice complement, the vegetables are so good cooked this way; one is tempted to dispense with the rest.

If you are limited by the size of your grill you may have to cook the vegetables in more than one batch. Also consider that some of the vegetables cook at different rates. Peppers need the least amount of time, followed by the eggplant, squash, and onions.

For the seasoned oil:

1 cup (250 ml) extra-virgin olive oil
2 garlic cloves, crushed
¼ cup (15 g) minced fresh basil or
  1 tablespoon minced fresh rosemary

For the vegetables:

2 (medium to large) eggplants, cut
  into rounds ½-in (13 mm) thick
2 to 4 assorted-color summer squash,
  depending on their size (if large, cut
  diagonally into slices ½-in [13 mm]
  thick; if small, slice lengthwise into
  halves or leave whole)
4 small whole red onions, or 1 large
  onion, quartered
2 to 4 sweet red or yellow peppers,
  halved and seeded
Salt and freshly ground black pepper

To make the seasoned oil: In a small bowl, mix the olive oil, garlic, and herbs and let them marinate at least 2 hours. (Refrigerate them if they are left to stand much longer).

To make the vegetables: Prepare the barbecue with charcoal and preheat. Meanwhile, place the vegetable slices on a cookie sheet and brush them with the seasoned oil. When the coals die down and are ready, spread them evenly around the bottom of the barbecue kettle. (If you are using a gas grill start it about 10 minutes before you want to cook the vegetables.) Place the vegetables oiled-side down on the grill. Brush the top sides of the vegetables with the oil and turn them when they are starting to brown.

Cooking time will vary in accordance with heat, distance from coals, and size and density of the vegetables. Over medium coals or gas grill on medium-low, expect average cooking time to be about 4 minutes on the first side and 3 minutes on the second side, but watch them carefully. Cook the vegetables until they are just tender, as they will fall apart if they are overcooked. Sprinkle with salt and pepper and serve. *Serves 4.*

Baked beets

In days of old the large keeper beets and carrots, winter staples, were roasted slowly over coals, intensifying their flavor and natural sweetness. Baking remains the best way for modern beet and carrot lovers to cook them; if you've never tried it, you'll be pleased with the results. Here are directions for preparing beets.

Figure that one large (4–5-in/10–13-g diameter) beet will feed two people

Scrub and trim the beets, but leave them whole. Set the greens aside.

Preheat the oven to 300°F (150°C). Place the roots in a casserole or baking dish and cover securely. (Do not add water.) Bake them for at least 1 hour, or until just tender. Just before the roots are ready, wash the beet greens, slice them thin, and steam them for about 3 minutes, or until tender.

To serve, peel the beets, if so desired, and slice them; serve hot on a platter with the greens. *Serves 2 as a side dish.*

Roast parsnips

Roast parsnips are an honored tradition in England, where they have been a part of the holiday festivities. John Downey, chef and owner of Downey's in Santa Barbara, provided this recipe. Serve it with roast turkey, roast pork, or beef.

6 medium parsnips
4 tablespoons meat drippings
** (turkey, pork, or beef) or butter**

Preheat the oven to 400°F (200°C).

Peel the parsnips and cut them into pieces approximately 3 inches (8 cm) by ³/₄ inch (19 mm). Blanch them in a pot of boiling water for 1 minute. Drain them well, spread them out, and pat dry. Heat an ovenproof frying pan, add the meat drippings, letting them get very hot, add the parsnips, and sauté for a few minutes over high heat. Place them in the oven to finish cooking—about 30 minutes. Drain them and serve. *Serves 6.*

Variation: Roast the parsnips right in the meat pan after blanching them. They will be tastier but will hold more fat. *Serves 6.*

Grilled radicchio and zucchini with agliata

This is a surprisingly delicious way to enjoy vegetables. Radicchio and zucchini have a luscious smoky flavor and sweetness when they're grilled. Serve the vegetables with grilled chicken, steak, or fish. For a vegetarian feast, serve it with polenta and grilled portobello mushrooms.

For the sauce:
1 garlic head and 3 minced cloves, divided
³/₄ cup (185 ml) and 3 tablespoons extra-virgin olive oil, divided
¹/₄ cup (65 ml) balsamic vinegar
2 cups (110 g) day-old Italian rustic bread, crust removed, cubed
2 tablespoons fresh Italian parsley, chopped
¹/₄ teaspoon salt plus extra
Freshly ground black pepper

For the vegetables:
4 small zucchini
1 large radicchio

To make the sauce: Preheat the oven to 350°F (175°C).

With a sharp knife cut off the top of the garlic head until the cloves are exposed. Place the garlic in a small baking dish and sprinkle on 1 tablespoon of the olive oil. Bake the garlic for 20 minutes, or until it's soft. Set it aside.

In a bowl mix the balsamic vinegar and ¹/₄ cup (65 ml) of water. Add the bread cubes and soak them for about 15 minutes or until they're very soft. Squeeze the liquid out of the bread and put the bread into a mixing bowl. Squeeze the roasted garlic from its paper onto the bread. Add one of the minced garlic cloves, and the parsley. Blend all the ingredients into a thick paste. Season with the salt and pepper. Stir in ³/₄ cup (190 ml) of olive oil, a few drops at a time, to make an emulsion. The oil will not be absorbed completely; a little oil on top is traditional.

To cook the vegetables: Cut the zucchini lengthwise and quarter the radicchio. Place them in a shallow baking dish.

Blend the remaining 2 minced garlic cloves with the remaining 2 tablespoons of olive oil and brush the zucchini and radicchio with the mixture. Season with salt and pepper. Let the vegetables marinate for at least 1 hour.

Grill the radicchio over a medium flame, using tongs to turn it often so each side blackens slightly and the vegetables are tender inside, about 10 to 12 minutes. At the same time grill the zucchini halves on both sides until they're golden and tender, about 10 to 12 minutes. Transfer them to a warm serving plate.

(Instead of grilling them, you may broil the radicchio and zucchini in the oven. Broil at 400°F [200°C] for 6 to 10 minutes, or until golden.)

Serve immediately and pass the agliata sauce for diners to serve themselves. *Serves 4.*

Spicy bean sprouts

Many Asian cultures enjoy bean sprout salads. This is a spicy Korean version.

For the dressing:
- 1 tablespoon vegetable oil
- 2 teaspoons hot sesame oil
- 1 tablespoon toasted sesame seeds, ground
- 2 garlic cloves, minced
- 2 scallions (green onions), finely chopped
- ¼ cup (65 ml) soy sauce
- 1 teaspoon sugar
- ½ teaspoon cayenne pepper
- Garnish: 1 teaspoon whole toasted sesame seeds

For the salad:
- 1 lb (500 g) fresh mung bean sprouts

To make the dressing: Combine all the dressing ingredients in a small jar, cover, and shake vigorously.

To make the salad: Carefully wash the bean sprouts. Bring 2 quarts (2 liters) of salted water to a rolling boil. Add the sprouts and cook them for 1 minute. Do not overcook, as the sprouts should remain crunchy. Drain and rinse with cold water. In a bowl, toss the sprouts with the dressing and chill for about 1 hour. Sprinkle with whole sesame seeds before serving. *Serves 4.*

Japanese greens with sesame dressing

Shungiku or chrysanthemum greens are easily grown in cool weather. When you don't have them in your garden they are usually available in Asian grocery stores. Cooked greens with a sesame dressing is a popular vegetable side dish in Japan. Serve the greens with grilled fish, rice, and one or two types of pickles for a typical Japanese meal.

For the dressing:
1 teaspoon toasted sesame seeds, ground
1 teaspoon sugar
2 tablespoons chicken stock
¹⁄₃ cup (85 ml) soy sauce

For the salad:
1 lb (500 g) shungiku greens
Garnish: 1 teaspoon toasted sesame seeds, whole

To make the dressing: Combine all the ingredients in a small jar, cover, and shake vigorously.

To make the salad: Wash the shungiku greens and remove any thick stems. Bring 2 quarts (2 liters) of water to a rolling boil. Add the greens and cook for 1 minute. Drain and rinse with cold water. Press the water from the shungiku and put into a bowl. Dress the greens with the sesame dressing and sprinkle with whole, toasted sesame seeds. *Serves 4.*

Spicy eggplant

This is a classic Indian treatment of eggplant filled with lots of fragrant spices. Serve with grilled meats, Indian flat bread or pita bread, and cucumber raita.

For the masala spice mixture:

1½ teaspoons ground coriander
    seeds
2 teaspoons ground cumin
½ teaspoon ground red pepper
1 bay leaf
⅛ teaspoon cinnamon
⅛ teaspoon freshly ground nutmeg
Dash of ground cloves
Dash of ground cardamom

For the eggplant:

1 lb (500 g) eggplant (2 medium)
1½ tablespoons vegetable oil
1 tablespoon butter
2 medium onions, finely chopped
Masala spice mixture (see above)
3 medium fresh tomatoes, peeled,
    seeded, and chopped
2 or 3 green chilies, seeded and
    chopped
Salt and freshly ground black pepper
1 tablespoon chopped fresh cilantro

Combine the spices and set aside. Preheat a gas, electric, or charcoal grill. Cut the eggplants in half lengthwise and cut scores into the flesh, without cutting through the skin. Rub the eggplant halves with a little vegetable oil and grill until the skin blackens and the eggplants are soft. Cool, then peel, and chop the flesh coarsely.

In a medium pot, heat the remaining vegetable oil and the butter and sauté the onions until they are golden. Add the masala spices and cook together for 1 minute. Add the tomatoes and green chilies and sauté for 3 more minutes. Remove and discard the bay leaf. Add the chopped eggplant and sauté until the mixture is dry and comes away from the sides of the pan. Add salt and freshly ground pepper to taste and garnish with the cilantro. Serve hot or at room temperature. *Serves 4.*

Classic broccoli raab

This variation on a traditional Italian recipe was developed by Joe Queirolo, garden manager of Mudd's Restaurant, in San Ramon, California, and my onetime garden manager. Joe serves the broccoli over orecchiette or polenta.

1 bunch broccoli raab
2 tablespoons extra-virgin olive oil
1 or 2 garlic cloves, minced
¼ cup (65 ml) white wine
Salt and freshly ground pepper
¼ cup (25 g) grated Pecorino-
    Romano cheese

Wash the broccoli raab and trim off or peel any coarse stems. Bring a big pot of salted water to a boil. Add the broccoli raab and boil for about 3 to 5 minutes, or until tender. Drain the broccoli raab and run it under cold water so that it will hold its color.

Meanwhile, heat the oil and sauté the garlic over medium heat until softened, about 1 minute. Add the broccoli raab and toss. Stir in the white wine and let the mixture reduce for 2 or 3 minutes, shaking the pan occasionally. Add salt and pepper to taste. Pour into a serving dish and sprinkle on the cheese; serve immediately. *Serves 4 as a side dish.*

Risotto-stuffed swiss chard

Large chard leaves are great for stuffing. Serve stuffed chard as a course by itself or as a side dish with meat, fish, and poultry.

2 tablespoons butter
1/2 medium onion, chopped
4 oz (125 g) prosciutto, chopped
1 portobello mushroom, or 6 button mushrooms, chopped
1 cup (225 g) arborio rice
1/2 cup (125 ml) dry white wine
3 to 4 cups (750 ml–1 liter) low-salt beef broth
1/4 cup (25 g) Parmesan cheese, grated
12 Swiss chard leaves
1/2 cup (125 ml) tomato sauce
1/2 cup (50 g) Gruyère cheese

In a heavy saucepan, melt the butter and sauté the onion, prosciutto, and mushrooms over medium heat until tender, about 10 minutes. Add the rice and stir to coat the rice evenly. Add the white wine and simmer, stirring, until the liquid has evaporated. Add the broth, 1 cup (250 ml) at a time, always stirring. Simmer for 20 to 30 minutes; rice should be al dente. Stir in the Parmesan cheese.

Preheat the oven to 350°F (175°C). Remove the thick lower part of the chard stalks. Steam the leaves for 2 minutes, or until they have wilted. Drain the leaves and rinse them under cold water. Drain them again and place the leaves on paper towels to absorb the moisture. Spoon approximately 2 tablespoons of the arborio mixture onto the middle of each leaf, putting less in smaller leaves. Fold the sides toward the center, then fold in the ends. Make sure the ends overlap to keep the filling secure. Place each package seam-side down in a shallow baking dish that has been brushed with a little olive oil. Spoon tomato sauce over each package. Sprinkle the stuffed chard leaves with the Gruyère and bake them for 20 minutes. Serve immediately. *Serves 4, three per person.*

Roasted potatoes with thyme and rosemary

In France, home vegetable gardens are alive and well. Called *potager* gardens, they give a small harvest of the family's favorite vegetables throughout the year. This side dish can be made throughout much of the year, as potatoes of all sizes and maturity are produced from spring through fall. So too there is a constant supply of leaves from the perennial herbs—rosemary and thyme. Young new potatoes take less time to cook than the more mature ones, so check new potatoes often to avoid overcooking them.

12 to 14 small potatoes, each about 1 1/2 in (4 cm) in diameter, or 5 large potatoes
4 garlic cloves, minced
3 tablespoons extra-virgin olive oil
1 tablespoon finely chopped fresh thyme
1 tablespoon finely chopped fresh rosemary
1/2 teaspoon salt
1/2 teaspoon freshly ground black pepper

Preheat the oven to 400°F (200°C).

Wash the potatoes (cut large ones into equal pieces about 1 1/2 in [4 cm] across). Place them on a cookie sheet. Mix the garlic with the olive oil and drizzle the mixture over the potatoes. Sprinkle on the thyme, rosemary, salt, and pepper. Stir so that the potatoes are evenly coated with the oil and seasonings. Distribute the potatoes evenly around the cookie sheet. Bake the potatoes until they are golden and crispy, 30–40 minutes. Stir or shake the cookie sheet a few times as the potatoes are cooking so that they will brown evenly and to prevent sticking. *Serves 4.*

Note: Many vegetables can be roasted in the same manner as the potatoes above. They include carrots, parsnips, beets, boiling onions, and leeks. Rosemary is a classic herbal flavoring, but a mix of Mediterranean herbs—oregano, thyme, savory, and tarragon—is splendid, as is a combination of sage and garlic. The key is to have the vegetables approximately the same size so they will be cooked at the same time.

Candied sweet potatoes

This recipe has its roots in the American South, but I grew up with it as part of our Massachusetts Thanksgiving feast and have continued the tradition in California for more than 30 years. Properly cooked sweet potatoes develop a chewy caramelized coating. For special occasions I double the recipe, using two large frying pans, since sweet potatoes are at their best just after they are cooked.

3 large sweet potatoes (about 2 lbs/1 kg)
3 tablespoons salted butter
3 tablespoons dark brown sugar
1 tablespoon dark corn syrup

Wash the sweet potatoes and cut them in half lengthwise. Bring a large kettle of water to a boil, add the sweet potatoes, and cover. Boil for about 20 minutes, or until just tender. Keep an eye on them, as they usually get tender at an uneven rate. Drain the cooked sweet potatoes, let them cool slightly, and then peel them.

In a very large frying pan, melt the butter over low heat. Add the brown sugar and then drizzle the corn syrup over the melted butter and stir together. Cut the sweet potato halves lengthwise and place them flat-side down in the pan in the butter mixture. Cook over medium to low heat for about 10 minutes, or until golden brown. Turn them over and cook for 5 to 10 more minutes, until both sides are golden. At this point you need to turn the pieces occasionally and watch carefully to prevent them from burning. Transfer them to a warm plate and serve immediately. *Serves 4.*

Cauliflower with red pepper soubise sauce

In France, a classic soubise traditionally has onions as the primary ingredient. Here, Jesse Cool, executive chef and owner of Flea Street Café in Menlo Park, California, has created a variation made with red peppers. She says of her recipe, "This pepper soubise is both delicious and beautiful. Try it with steamed broccoli too; both can serve as an elegant appetizer or side dish."

1 cup (150 g) chopped yellow onions

2 cups (270 g) chopped roasted sweet red peppers

2 tablespoons olive oil

Cayenne, salt, and freshly ground black pepper

1 six-in (15-cm) head of cauliflower (about 1½ lbs/725 g)

In a large sauté pan, cook the onions and peppers in olive oil until very soft, about 25 minutes. Remove and purée in a blender or food processor. Stir in a little water if the mixture is too thick, add the seasonings, and keep the sauce warm.

Meanwhile, cut the cauliflower head into florets. Bring 1 inch (2.5 cm) of water to a boil in a steamer. Put florets in a steamer basket and steam for about 6 minutes or until the cauliflower is just tender.

To serve, pour about ⅓ cup (85 ml) of the pepper sauce on each of 4 warm plates. Put ¼ of the cauliflower on each plate. Drizzle the rest of the pepper sauce over each serving of cauliflower. *Serves 4 to 6.*

Creamed onions

Fresh creamed onions have been a holiday staple for eons. While they are great with turkey, try them other times of the year with other roasts or as part of a vegetable medley.

24 small white onions, peeled (about 1¼ lbs/625 g)
4 tablespoons salted butter
3 tablespoons all-purpose flour
2 cups (500 ml) low-fat milk
½ teaspoon salt
¼ teaspoon freshly ground black pepper
¼ teaspoon freshly grated nutmeg
Garnish: paprika

Boil the onions in 2 cups (500 ml) of water, uncovered, for 20 minutes, or until tender. The onions are done when you can insert a fork easily. Drain the cooking water into a bowl and reserve. You should have approximately ⅓ cup (85 ml) of cooking water left. Set the onions aside and keep them warm. In a heavy-bottomed saucepan, melt the butter and stir in the flour with a wire whisk. Cook this mixture over low heat for about 2 minutes, constantly stirring. Add the reserved cooking water and continue to stir. Add the milk, and bring the sauce to a boil while whisking. Lower the heat, and simmer, stirring, for 3 to 5 minutes more. Add the salt, pepper, and nutmeg. Pour the sauce over the onions and sprinkle liberally with paprika. Serve immediately. *Serves 4.*

Leeks and new potatoes with savory cream

The herb savory brings out the richness of vegetables. Nowhere is it more evident than in this voluptuous dish in which it flavors leeks, cream, and potatoes.

1 pint (500 ml) whipping cream

4 (3-in/8-cm) sprigs of fresh winter savory, divided

14 to 16 new potatoes (2–2½ in [5–6 cm] in diameter), washed but not peeled

1 teaspoon salt

10 to 12 young leeks, ½ to 1 in (13 mm–2.5 cm) in diameter, or 4 large leeks

1 tablespoon butter

¼ teaspoon nutmeg

Salt and freshly ground black pepper

Garnish: fresh sprigs of winter savory

Put the cream and 3 sprigs of the savory in a saucepan and bring it to a boil. Remove from the heat and let the cream steep for about 1 hour.

In another saucepan, boil the potatoes in water with salt and the remaining sprig of savory until just tender, approximately 20 minutes.

Clean the leeks by partially cutting them lengthwise and flushing them with water. Cut the white parts diagonally in pieces approximately 2 inches (5 cm) long. (For large leeks, cut into 1-inch/2.5-cm pieces.) If the lower portions of the green leaves are tender, slice them as

well. (Use tough green tops to make stock.) Sauté the leeks in butter for 5 minutes, or until tender, and set aside.

Remove the savory sprigs from the cream and discard. Bring the cream to a boil and reduce until about half remains, approximately 6 to 10 minutes. Season with nutmeg, salt, and pepper.

To serve, reheat leeks if necessary. Arrange the leeks on part of a serving plate. Drain the potatoes and place them on the other side of the plate. Pour the reduced cream over the leeks and potatoes and garnish with savory sprigs. *Serves 4 as a side dish.*

Red, white, and blue potato salad

This potato salad is an eye-catching addition to luncheons, particularly around the Fourth of July and elections. If you have no blue potatoes in your garden, they are occasionally available from specialty produce markets. Select only the deep blue-fleshed potatoes as the light and medium blue-fleshed ones turn an unappetizing gray when boiled. Blue-fleshed potatoes can be used in any potato salad recipe, but the color is best featured when a clear dressing is used.

For the dressing:

2 tablespoons rich chicken stock

¼ cup (65 ml) white wine vinegar

2 tablespoons dry white wine or white vermouth

Salt and freshly ground pepper to taste

½ cup (125 ml) extra-virgin olive oil

1 tablespoon chopped parsley

1 tablespoon fresh chopped tarragon

For the salad:

4 medium white boiling potatoes

4 medium deep blue-fleshed potatoes (or 2 blue- and 2 red-fleshed potatoes)

½ cup (90 g) thinly sliced red bell peppers

½ teaspoon freshly ground pepper

To make the dressing: In a small bowl mix the chicken stock, vinegar, wine, salt, and pepper until the salt is dissolved. Slowly, whisk in the olive oil. Add the parsley and the tarragon and stir well to combine.

To make the salad: In two separate pots, boil the 2 or 3 colors of potatoes for 20 to 30 minutes until just barely tender when stuck with a fork. While still warm, peel the potatoes and slice them into ¼-inch- (6-mm-) thick slices.

Place the potatoes in a large salad bowl, alternating layers of blue and white potatoes with the red peppers. Pour the dressing over the still-warm potatoes and sprinkle with the pepper. Toss gently so the dressing gets evenly dispersed and the potatoes don't fall apart. (If the potatoes are overcooked or the mixing is too vigorous it will cause the separate colors of potatoes to mingle and the result will be a muddy looking salad.)

Let the salad sit for 3 or 4 hours so the flavors will meld. Serve the salad at room temperature or chilled. *Serves 4 to 6.*

Purée of celeriac

Celeriac is a beloved French vegetable with a nutty, celery taste. The most common recipe for celeriac is *céleri-rave rémoulade*, an appetizer of celeriac cut into matchsticks and mixed with herbs and mustard. Here we have instead a creamy purée that is served warm to accompany a pork roast or braised lamb.

2 large celeriac bulbs (about 2 lbs/1 kg)

2 teaspoons fresh lemon juice

1 tablespoon butter

2 tablespoons heavy cream

¼ teaspoon salt

Freshly ground black pepper

Dash of nutmeg

Peel the celeriac and cut into 1½-inch (4-cm) pieces. In a medium saucepan, bring 1½ cups (375 ml) water to a boil. Add the lemon juice and celeriac and simmer, covered, until the vegetable is soft, about 15 minutes. Drain. Purée the celeriac in a blender or food processor. Return the celeriac to the saucepan and add the butter, cream, salt, pepper, and nutmeg. Mix with a wire whisk until the seasonings have blended and the purée is smooth. Warm up the purée and serve. *Serves 4 as a side dish.*

Drinks
and
desserts

Candied flowers

Baby roses, Johnny-jump-ups, violets, violas, scented geraniums, orange blossoms, edible pea blossoms (not sweet peas, which are poisonous), and borage are all particularly well suited to candying.

Use candied flowers to decorate cakes, cookies, ice cream, and hors d'oeuvres. Wedding cakes are stunning covered with candied roses, and salmon canapés are dramatic decorated with candied pea blossoms. For an Art Deco presentation, cover a cake with marzipan icing, wrap it with blue French ribbon, and create a cluster of matte-finish, candied blue pansies.

In the cool of the morning on a dry day, select and cut flowers that are perfectly shaped and newly opened. Keep enough of their stems so you can put them in water and later hold them comfortably. Wash the flowers a few hours before working with them so they will be dry.

To candy flowers, you need a small paintbrush, a bowl, cake rack, fork, finely ground granulated sugar (sometimes called bartenders' sugar or superfine sugar), and an egg white.

In a small bowl, beat the egg white only slightly. Holding a flower by its stem, gently paint the petals with a light coating of egg white, thoroughly covering the front and back because any part of the petal not covered will wither and discolor. Sprinkle the flowers with sugar, making sure to cover both sides of the petals thoroughly. An alternative method is to use a paste mixture of confectioners' sugar and a little egg white. This mixture gives a matte finish to citrus blossoms and large flowers like dark-colored pansies. Paint this mixture on both sides of the petals.

When your flower is completely sugared, lay it on a cake rack and spread the petals in a natural position. After an hour or two move the flowers around so the petals won't stick to the rack. Put the flowers in a warm, dry place (I use my gas oven, with just the heat from its pilot light) or in a food dehydrator set on low. After a few days they should be fully dry; store them in a sealed tin. Some of the flowers will become deformed; discard them or break them up to use as a confetti. You can use your candied flowers immediately, but if you store them in a dry place, most varieties will keep for up to a year.

Left: When you candy flowers, if you use confectioners' instead of granulated sugar you can achieve a matte finish on the flowers, giving them a delicate, old-fashioned look. This cake has been garnished with yellow pansies that were treated in this manner. **Above left:** To candy violets or other edible flowers, first give them a light coating of egg white with a paintbrush, being careful to completely cover the petals. With your fingers, lightly sprinkle extra-fine granulated sugar over the petals. Dry them on a rack in a very warm, dry place for a few days or in a dehydrator until firm. Once the flowers are dry, put them in a flat, dry container. Use the flowers to decorate cakes and cookies. **Above right:** Any broken pieces of candied flowers can be used to sprinkle on confections as you would confetti, as shown here.

Apricot pandoro

Nearly thirty years ago when we moved into our house in California's Santa Clara Valley we found the remnants of an apricot orchard—four trees. I discovered lots of great recipes for apricots including apricot brandy, glazes for ham, nectar, and this recipe for using our dried apricots.

This lovely bread is a variation on the traditional holiday bread from Verona, Italy, made with raisins and candied fruits. When served as dessert it is usually accompanied by a bowl of whipped cream or mascarpone cheese. It's also delicious toasted for breakfast.

This particular recipe only works well with rapid-rise yeast, not standard yeast. Using an instant-read thermometer eliminates a lot of the guesswork. (See photo on page 190.)

3 ¼ to 3 ½ cups (360–370 g) un-
    bleached all-purpose flour
1 teaspoon salt
⅓ cup (75 g) sugar
1 package (7 g) rapid-rising yeast
Zest of 1 lemon
½ cup (125 ml) warm water
2 teaspoons vanilla extract
2 teaspoons apricot or other fruit
    brandy
4 tablespoons butter, cut into small
    pieces
2 eggs, at room temperature
⅓ cup (50 g) chopped dried apricots
Garnish: confectioners' sugar

Blend 3 cups (340 g) of the flour with the salt, sugar, yeast, and lemon zest in the bowl of a heavy-duty stationary mixer, fitted with a paddle attachment. Heat the water to 120 to 130°F (50–55°C).

Add the vanilla, apricot brandy, and butter to the water. Add the liquid ingredients to the dry ingredients and beat until smooth. Add both eggs and beat 1 minute longer. Replace the mixer's paddle with its dough hook and use it to knead the dough, gradually adding the remaining flour until the dough is smooth and silky and pulls away from the sides of the bowl. Just before you finish kneading add the chopped apricots.

Generously butter the pandoro pan. Push the dough down into the pan, cover with plastic wrap, and let rise in a warm place for 1 ½ to 2 hours or until it comes within 1 inch (2.5 cm) of the top of the mold. After the dough has risen sufficiently, preheat the oven to 350°F (175°C). Bake for 1 hour, or until golden brown and the internal temperature registers 190°F (85°C) on an instant-read thermometer (or until a cake tester inserted into thickest part of the bread comes out clean).

Cool the pandoro in the pan for 10 to 15 minutes before inverting it onto a wire rack. When almost cool, place the pandoro on a serving plate and dust with confectioners' sugar. *Serves 6 to 8.*

Note: The cake on page 190 was baked in a traditional fancy star-shaped mold. Similar molds can be purchased from mail-order cooking supply houses such as Sur La Table (800-243-0852; www.surlatable.com) or King Arthur Flour (800-827-6836; www.kingarthurflour.com). You can also use any mold that will hold a yeasted bread recipe calling for 3 ½ cups (400 g) of flour.

Baked apples with cherries and hazelnuts

Baked apples are one of my favorite treats and this recipe beats all the others I have ever had. It's not too sweet and the strong tart apple flavor contrasts with the sweet creamy whipped cream. Most recipes call for raisins but I especially like it with dried cherries or cranberries.

3 oz (100 g) filbert nuts
6 large baking apples, such as Jonagold, Newtown Pippin, Rome Beauty, Granny Smith, or other firm cooking apple
3 tablespoons finely chopped orange zest
1/3 cup (85 ml) orange juice
2 tablespoons brown sugar
1 tablespoon butter, melted
1/4 cup (45 g) dried sweet cherries, cranberries, or raisins
1 cup (250 ml) of heavy cream, whipped
Garnish: thin strips of orange zest

Preheat oven to 350°F (175°C). Place the filberts on a cookie sheet and bake for 10 minutes. Remove the filberts from the oven, place them on a clean dish towel and rub them to remove most of their skins. Place the peeled nuts in a blender and grind until they are a fine powder.

Core the apples and set them aside. In a small bowl, mix together the orange zest, orange juice, brown sugar, butter, filberts, and cherries.

Stuff each apple with 1/6 of this mixture. Place the stuffed apples in a baking pan and bake for approximately 30 minutes or until the they are tender when pierced with a knife. Remove them from the baking dish; place an apple on each of six serving plates and garnish with orange zest strips. Serve with whipped cream. *Serves 6.*

Fig needhams

The name of this cookie is actually an inside joke. I grew up in Needham, Massachusetts, and my school's archrival in football was Newton High School. I bet you these cookies will be better than any store-bought ones you ever had.

For the filling:
1 lb (500 g) of fresh figs, chopped
2 tablespoons water
2 to 4 tablespoons sugar

For the cookies:
1 cup (225 g) butter
1 cup (200 g) brown sugar
2 egg yolks
3 tablespoons milk
2 teaspoons vanilla
2 1/2 cups (280 g) unbleached flour
2 teaspoons cream of tartar
1 teaspoon baking soda
1/2 teaspoon salt

To make the filling: Place the figs in a saucepan with the water and add sugar to taste (start with 2 tablespoons). Cook over low heat, stirring occasionally, until thick. *Makes approximately 3/4 cup (190 ml) filling. Any extra filling can be frozen.*

To make the cookies: Preheat the oven to 350 °F (175°C). Cream the butter and sugar. Add the egg yolks, milk, and vanilla and beat well. Sift together the dry ingredients and add them to the mixture. Chill the dough for at least an hour.

On a well-floured board, roll out the dough to 1/8 inch (3 mm) thick. Use a round cookie cutter to cut the rolled-out dough into circles. Place 1/2 teaspoon of the fig filling on half of the dough circles. Cut small holes in the center of the remaining rounds and place them on top of these dough circles, forming sandwiches.

Press the edges of each cookie together with a fork. Bake on an ungreased cookie sheet for 10 to 12 minutes or until slightly golden. *Makes approximately 2 dozen cookies, depending on the diameter of the cookie cutter used.*

Rhubarb and strawberry cobbler

This traditional rhubarb cobbler is surprisingly light and creamy.

For the filling:

6 to 8 stalks rhubarb, cut into ¹/₂-in (13-mm) pieces (about 3 cups/360 g)

²/₃ cup (150 g) sugar

1 tablespoon orange or lemon zest

1 tablespoon salted butter

1 tablespoon all-purpose flour

3 cups (500 g) sliced strawberries

For the batter:

1³/₄ cups (195 g) flour

1 tablespoon baking powder

¹/₂ teaspoon salt

6 tablespoons salted butter, chilled

¹/₂ cup (115 g) sugar plus 2 table-spoons, divided

³/₄ cup (170 ml) half-and-half

2 tablespoons grated orange or lemon zest, divided

1 cup (250 ml) heavy cream whipped with 1 tablespoon sugar (optional)

To make the filling: In a saucepan over medium heat, cook the rhubarb, sugar, and 1 tablespoon orange zest until the rhubarb begins to juice, about 2 minutes. Add the butter and flour and bring to a boil while stirring. Cook for about 1 minute. Add the sliced strawberries. Remove from heat and pour the fruit mixture into a deep 10-inch (25-cm) pie dish.

To make the batter: Preheat the oven to 425°F (220°C). In a large bowl, sift together the flour, baking powder, and salt. Cut the butter into small pieces. With a fork or a pastry cutter, cut the chilled butter until the mixture resembles coarse crumbs. Add ¹/₂ cup (125 g) of the sugar and blend. Slowly incorporate the half-and-half with a fork. Spoon the dough over the fruit mixture in the pie dish. Mix 2 tablespoons sugar and the remaining orange zest and sprinkle it over the top. Bake for 25 to 30 minutes, or until golden brown. Cool slightly and serve with or without whipped cream. *Serves 6.*

Golden chard dessert tart

It is not unusual in Italy to have ricotta cheese in a tart. This version is enriched with golden grapes and chard. It makes a lovely, not-too-sweet finale to a meal.

For the crust:

2 cups (220 g) all-purpose flour
$\frac{1}{2}$ cup (75 g) ground blanched almonds
$\frac{1}{4}$ cup (60 g) sugar
$\frac{3}{4}$ cup (170 g) butter, cut in small pieces, at room temperature
1 egg yolk

For the filling:

3 eggs
15 oz (425 g) low-fat ricotta cheese
$\frac{1}{4}$ cup (65ml) honey
$\frac{1}{4}$ cup (65 ml) dry white wine
Dash of grated nutmeg
2 cups (75 g) finely chopped golden chard leaves and tender stems (about 5 medium leaves)
1 tablespoon chopped fresh mint
1$\frac{1}{2}$ cups (255 g) grated yellow squash (about 1 large squash)

To make the crust: In the bowl of a stand mixer combine the flour, almonds, and sugar and stir. Add the butter and the egg yolk to the dry ingredients. Using the paddle attachment, beat on medium speed until the mixture is the texture of coarse corn meal. Gather into a ball, wrap in plastic and refrigerate for 15 minutes.

Preheat the oven to 375°F (190°C). Press the dough evenly into a 9-inch (23-cm) tart or pie pan. Cover it with parchment paper or aluminum foil and chill the crust for 15 minutes. Before prebaking the shell, fill its cavity with dry beans or rice to weigh down the crust so it will not bubble up. Bake for 10 minutes. Remove the paper and the beans or rice used as weights and reserve.

To prepare the filling: In a mixing bowl, blend the eggs with the cheese, honey, wine, and nutmeg. Then fold in the chard, mint, and squash. Pour the filling into the warm pie shell and bake it on the middle shelf of the oven for 50 minutes or until golden brown. The filling should be set when a toothpick inserted in the center comes out clean. *Serves 6 to 8.*

Carrot pie

Today Americans think of vegetable pies as being pumpkin or squash, traditionally enjoyed as holiday desserts. However, in Colonial days all vegetable pies, including carrot pie, were similarly spiced and were enjoyed as part of a large farm lunch or supper, not as dessert. Who knows, you may make this pie and start a new family tradition—pie for lunch.

1¼ lbs (625 g) carrots
¾ cup (170 g) white or ¾ cup (150 g) brown sugar
1 cup (250 ml) milk or cream
1 teaspoon cinnamon
½ teaspoon ginger
¼ teaspoon freshly ground nutmeg
⅛ teaspoon allspice or cloves
3 eggs
1 unbaked 9-in (23-cm) pie shell

Wash the carrots and peel the skins if they are tough. Slice the carrots and steam them until tender. (You should have about 4 cups/630 g of sliced carrots.) Purée them in a blender or food processor.

Preheat the oven to 425°F (220°C).

Add the remaining ingredients, except the pie shell, to the carrots in a mixing bowl and blend until smooth and evenly mixed. (You may have to do so in two batches, depending on the blender's capacity. If so, mix the batches together before pouring the purée into the pie shell.) Pour the purée into the pie shell. Bake for 15 minutes. Reduce heat to 350°F (175°C) and bake for 45 more minutes, or until set. Let the pie cool for at least 30 minutes before serving. *Serves 6.*

Lavender shortbreads

Shortbread cookies lend themselves to all sorts of special flavor variations. Here, I use lavender, but rose geraniums would be tasty too. Shortbread cookie stamps are available from some specialty baking-supply houses.

2 cups (455 g) unsalted butter, room temperature

1 cup (225 g) Lavender Sugar (see recipe, page 38)

½ teaspoon salt

4 cups (440 g) all-purpose flour

2 teaspoons dried lavender blossoms

To make the shortbread: Using the paddle attachment on a stand mixer, blend the butter, lavender sugar, and salt on a low to medium speed until light and fluffy, about 10 minutes. Work in the flour gradually, scraping the bowl occasionally to blend all the ingredients well. Mix in the lavender blossoms. Shape the dough into a ball, wrap it in plastic wrap, and refrigerate it for at least 2 hours.

To shape the shortbread: If you're using a cookie stamp, cut the dough into golf-ball-size pieces. Roll each piece into a ball with your floured hands, then press it with the lightly floured stamp. Gently remove the stamp and place the formed dough on a cookie sheet lined with parchment paper.

If you don't have a stamp, roll out the dough on a floured board to about ½ inch (13 mm) thick. Using a cookie cutter or a 3-inch- (8-cm-) diameter water glass, cut out circles and place them on a parchment-lined cookie sheet. Score each cookie with the tines of a fork a few times, making a pleasing pattern. You can also cut the dough into equal rectangles instead of circles.

Refrigerate the formed cookies for 30 minutes before baking them. Preheat the oven to 300°F (150°C). Bake the shortbread for 25 to 30 minutes, or until it is pale golden but not brown. *Makes about 2 dozen cookies.*

Herbed vodka

Herb and flower vodkas have either herbs, spices, or fruits added to them. Serve them ice cold. Here is a flavored vodka recipe from Carole Saville, author and herb maven.

2 cups (500 ml) good-quality vodka
1 tablespoon sweet woodruff leaves, or 2 tablespoons fresh lemongrass stalks cut diagonally from the white portion of the base into ¹/₄-in (6-mm) slices, or 1 teaspoon coarsely chopped, fresh English lavender leaves

Combine the herbs and vodka in a very clean wide-mouth pint jar. Seal the jar and allow the mixture to steep for 24 hours at room temperature. Taste for flavoring. If a stronger flavor is desired, infuse the herbs for another 24 hours, or until the flavor suits you. Strain the mixture through a cheesecloth-lined funnel, and pour it into a very clean, decorative pint bottle. Seal tightly with a cork or cap. Store the flavored vodka in the freezer. *Makes 2 cups (500 ml).*

Melon cooler

In a hot climate such as Mexico's, cool, refreshing fruit drinks are a must—a part of everyday life. Often such Mexican drinks include melons, either watermelon or cantaloupe, from the garden. This version includes tequila but rum could be used, or it could be made without any alcohol at all—it would be equally delicious. The following proportions I find pleasing and not too sweet, but you may want to add more sugar or lime juice. I make it light on the tequila so I can enjoy more than one glass.

¹/₂ small watermelon, large seeds removed, cubed
1 to 2 tablespoons sugar
Juice of 1¹/₂ limes
2 shots tequila
Garnish: spearmint leaves

Put the watermelon cubes in a blender or food processor bowl, add 1 cup (250 ml) of water, and blend until fairly smooth. (You may have to do this in more than one batch.) Strain the juice to remove the seeds. (This is usually necessary even with seedless watermelons, as they have small white vestigial seeds.) Add the sugar and lime juice, stir, and adjust the flavorings to suit your taste. The mixture can be refrigerated for a few hours at this point.

Before serving, add the tequila and stir. Chill 4 large glasses, then fill them half full of shaved ice. Pour the watermelon mixture over the ice and garnish each glass with mint leaves. *Makes about 1 quart (1 liter).*

Rose petal sorbet

Micheal Isles, chef/instructor in Chico, California, created this fabulous treat. Make the syrup at least two days before making the sorbet.

1 cup (250 ml) rose petal syrup (see recipe below)
1 bottle of late harvest Gewürtzraminer grape juice
4 perfect, large rose blossoms
1 egg white

A day before serving, combine the syrup and grape juice in an ice cream maker. Follow the manufacturer's directions for making sorbet. Once the sorbet is done, freeze it in an airtight container for 24 hours. You can get away with only 3 hours as an absolute minimum.

To serve, choose four perfect, large roses, remove the centers, spread them open, and secure them to the middle of the plates or dishes with a little egg white. Just before serving, place a scoop of sorbet in each rose. The sorbet may also be served in sherbet glasses or floating in champagne in fancy long-stemmed goblets. *Serves 4 to 6.*

Rose petal syrup

This versatile syrup can be used on crepes or pancakes, drizzled over sponge cake, or used in sorbets. My favorite roses to use are 'Belle of Portugal,' 'Abraham Darby,' and the spicy Rosa rugosa alba. Try your own varieties for flavor. Some are sensational, others metallic or bitter tasting. If the white bases of the petals are bitter, remove them.

2 cups (200 g) rose petals
²/₃ cup (150 g) sugar

Wash the petals and dry them in a salad spinner. Check for insects. Chop the petals very fine. In a medium saucepan, bring 1 cup (250 ml) of water to a boil and stir in the sugar. When the sugar is melted, add the petals. Remove the syrup from the heat and cover it tightly. Let it steep overnight.

Taste the syrup the next day, and if the flavor is not strong enough, reheat the syrup, add more petals, and let it steep overnight again. You can store the syrup in the refrigerator for up to 2 weeks—freeze it for longer storage. *Makes 1 cup (250 ml).*

Caution: Use only roses that have not been sprayed with commercial chemicals. Diners allergic to sulfur should be particularly careful, as organic gardeners often use sulfur to control rose diseases.

Persimmon smoothie

This low-fat smoothie is rich with flavor and perfect for a nutritious breakfast or a light lunch. Frozen persimmons can be substituted for fresh ones. If you do this, peel but don't defrost each persimmon; cut it into 4 or 5 pieces and eliminate the ice cubes in the recipe. This smoothie can also be made with bananas or peaches instead of persimmons.

1/2 cup (115 g) nonfat plain yogurt
1 1/2 to 2 tablespoons honey
1 cup (250 ml) nonfat milk or soy milk
2 'Fuyu' persimmons or 1 soft-ripe 'Hachiya' persimmon, peeled (remove seeds if there are any)
1/2 teaspoon vanilla
Dash of cinnamon
2 ice cubes
Garnish: a dollop of yogurt, slices of persimmon

Place all ingredients in a blender and process on medium speed for about 30 seconds, or until the ice cubes or frozen persimmons are crushed. Pour the mixture into a tall shake glass or 2 tumblers. Garnish with small dollops of yogurt and slices of persimmon if desired. *Makes 2 1/2 cups (625 ml).*

May wine bowl

This recipe is from Rose Marie Nichols McGee of Nichols Garden Nursery in Albany, Oregon, and it is a variation on the traditional libation from Germany. Germans use this traditional punch to celebrate May Day. In Germany sweet woodruff grows wild in the woods and is collected before it flowers, to capture the best taste. Germans use only wilted or dry sweet woodruff and add champagne or sparkling water.

5 bottles Moselle or Riesling wine
2 large handfuls sweet woodruff, cleaned
1 cup (250 ml) brandy
1 cup (225 g) sugar
A large ring mold of ice
1 cup (200 g) strawberries, Alpine or wild, if available

Pour 2 bottles of the wine into a large jar or crock, add 2 large handfuls of dry or wilted sweet woodruff, cover and refrigerate, and let stand for 3 days. Strain the infused wine into a large punch bowl and add the remaining 3 bottles of wine and the brandy, sugar, and ice. Add the strawberries to the bowl and decorate around the base of the bowl with sweet woodruff. *Serves about 20.*

Chamomile cooler

Chamomile is most beloved as a soothing herb tea. The following is my onetime gardener Wendy Krupnick's iced variation that helps cool a hot day.

1 heaping tablespoon dried German chamomile
1 heaping tablespoon crushed, dried spearmint or peppermint leaves
1 quart (1 liter) apple juice
1 tablespoon lemon juice (optional)

Garnish: lemon slices and fresh mint leaves

Place the herbs in an ovenproof jar or pot. Pour 3 cups (750 ml) of boiling water over the herbs, cover the pot, and let it steep for 15 to 20 minutes. Strain the tea into a large pitcher. Add the apple juice and lemon juice (if desired) and chill. Serve over ice and garnish with lemon slices and mint leaves. *Serves 6.*

Lemongrass tea

Lemongrass makes a sprightly herb tea. Here, it is made with palm sugar (available from Asian grocery stores), but it is also pleasant with standard white sugar. For a variation try adding a little chopped ginger root. Harvest or purchase 3 or 4 stalks of lemongrass. Use the bottom 3 or 4 inches (8–10 cm) for this tea.

¹⁄₂ cup (35 g) thinly sliced fresh
  lemongrass
2 to 3 tablespoons palm sugar (or
  white sugar)
1 quart (1 liter) cold water

Place the lemongrass and the palm sugar in the bottom of a teapot. Bring the water to a boil and pour it into the teapot over the lemongrass. Let the tea steep for at least 10 minutes. Pour the tea through a strainer and into teacups. *Serves 4.*

Chrysanthemum tea

This tea is famous in China and often served with dim sum.

4 tablespoons dried chrysanthemum
  flowers (shungiku)
1 quart (1 liter) cold water

Place the dried chrysanthemum flowers (shungiku) in the bottom of a teapot. Bring the water to a boil and pour it over the chrysanthemum flowers. Let the tea steep for at least 10 minutes. Pour the tea through a strainer and into tea cups. *Serves 4.*

Complete recipe list

Index by produce

Almond: Curry, golden chicken, 151; Dessert tart, golden chard, 197; Mole verde (green mole), 37; Salad, Jody's sprout, 54

Apple: Apples, baked, 195; Cabbage, red, braised, 165; Chamomile cooler, 203; Pork, roast, with fennel stuffing, 155

Apricot: Pandoro, apricot, 194

Artichoke: Bread pudding, savory, 110; Pain bagna (French-style sandwich), 115; Pizza, spring 112

Arugula: Penne with arugula, 112; Pizza, spring, 112; Salad, basic garden, 43; Salad, mesclun, 43; Salad, wild party, 45

Asparagus: Asparagus with hollandaise sauce, 175; Salad, crab and asparagus, 71; Soup, spring vegetable, with dumplings, 85

Avocado: Burritos, bean, 117; Salad, Oriana's cabbage, 51; Soup, tortilla, 84; Tacos, kaleidoscope, 118

Basil: Basil in Parmesan, 32; Chili, garden, 141; Fettuccine with fresh marinara sauce, 114; Flower canapés, 88; Herb blend, summer essence, 23; Lasagna, roasted pepper, 125; Omelet, squash blossom, 106; Pain bagna (French-style sandwich), 115; Peppers, grilled, red and gold, 171; Salad dressing, sundried tomato, 28; Salad, garden bouquet, 46; Salad, tomato and basil, 67; Vegetable marinade, 25; Vegetables, barbecued, 177; Zucchini blossoms, stuffed, 99

Thai: Salad rolls, Vietnamese, 134–135

Bay leaf: Bouquet garni, 22; Cabbage, red, braised, 165; Gumbo, classic, 142; Eggplant, spicy, 182; Herbes de Provence, 24; Herbes de Provence à la Bouterin, 24; Lamb, gardener's spring, 137; Rice, fennel, with pistachios, 131; Sandwiches, pork shoulder, 136–137; Soup, spring vegetable, with dumplings, 85

Beans: Beans, refried, 34; Burritos, bean, 117; Chili, garden, 141; Huevos rancheros, 107

Black: Chili, black bean and chicken, 141

Fava: Beans, Italian-style, 171; Fava beans with tomatoes, 163

Green: Salad, garden celebration, 61

Haricots verts (filet beans): Haricots verts, 172

Kidney: Beans, baked, with pork, 145

Lima: Succotash, 161

Pigeon peas: Soup, Thai chicken, 81

Pinto: Beans, refried, 34

Romano: Beans, Italian-style, 171; Salad, romano bean, with grilled tuna, 53

Snap: Salade niçoise, 68

Wax: Salad, garden celebration, 61

Yard-long: Gado-gado, 121; Vegetable rolls, Japanese, beef and pork, 138

See also Sprouts, bean

Beets: Beets, baked, 178; Salad, garden celebration, 61

Begonia, tuberous: Dip, citrus, for begonia blossoms, 87

Bitter melon: Stir-fry, bitter melon with beef, 146

Blueberry: Pancakes, true-blue blueberry, 108

Bok choy: Salad, wild party, 45

Borage: Herb blend, fresh flavor, 23; Salad, garden bouquet, 46

Broccoli: Curry, Thai red vegetable, 120

Broccoli raab: Broccoli raab, classic, 182

Brussels sprouts: Brussels sprouts with cream and nuts, 168

Burdock: Vegetable rolls, Japanese, beef and pork, 138

Burnet: Herb blend, tangy, 23

Cabbage: Beerocks, 144; Cabbage, red, braised, 165; New England boiled dinner, 152; Salad, garden celebration, 61; Salad, Oriana's cabbage, 51; Slaw, rainbow, 51; Soup, wonton dumpling, with oriental chives, 78

Chinese: Curry, Thai red vegetable, 120; Gado-gado, 121; Noodles, Japanese, 123

Calendula: Flower canapés, 88; Salad, garden bouquet, 46; Salad, spinach and watercress, 54

Cantaloupe: Melon and Prosciutto Appetizer, 88

Carrot: Bouquet garni, 22; Carrots with chervil butter, 164; Chili, black bean and chicken, 141; Curry, golden chicken, 151; Curry, Thai red vegetable, 120; Daikon, pickled, and carrots, 30; Gado-gado, 121; Lamb, gardener's spring, 137; New England boiled dinner, 152; Noodles, Japanese, 123; Pie, carrot, 198; Salad dressing, sun-dried tomato, 28; Slaw, rainbow, 51; Soup, fancy carrot and onion, 87; Soup, miso, 80; Soup, spring vegetable, with dumplings, 85; Soup, Thai chicken, 81; Soup, wonton dumpling, with oriental chives, 78; Stir-fry, carrot and garlic, 169; Summer vegetables, Grandma Alice's, 159; Tempura, vegetable, 101; Vegetable rolls, Japanese, beef and pork, 138

Cauliflower: Cauliflower with red pepper soubise sauce, 185

Celeriac: Celeriac, purée of, 189

Celery: Bouquet garni, 22; Chili, black bean and chicken, 141; Gumbo, classic, 142; Noodles, Japanese, 123; Soup, spring vegetable, with dumplings, 85; Soup, Thai chicken, 81

Chamomile, German: Chamomile cooler, 203

Chard: Dessert tart, golden chard, 197; Salad, basic garden, 43; Salad, Jody's sprout, 54; Salad, riot of color, 48; Slaw, rainbow, 51

Chard, Swiss: Swiss chard, risotto-stuffed, 183

Chayote: Chayote sauté with chilies, 158

Cherries, sweet: Apples, baked, 195

Chervil: Carrots with chervil butter, 164; Fines herbes, 22; Herb blend, classic mesclun, 23; Lamb, gardener's spring, 137; Salad dressing, garden ranch, 27; Salad, mesclun, 43

Chives: Bread pudding, savory, 110; Butter, nasturtium, 29; Butter, chive blossom, 29; Fines herbes, 22; Greens, hearty, with pears, 58; Herb blend, fresh flavor, 23; Omelet, squash blossom, 106; Pancakes, potato, with chives, 94; Potatoes, savory mashed, 167; Salad dressing, garden ranch, 27; Salad, garden bouquet, 46; Salad, wild party, 45; Tart, golden tomato, 116; Torta, salmon, cream cheese, and chive, 102; Vichyssoise, lavender-tinted, 77

Chives, oriental: Herb blend, Asian, 23; Salad rolls, Vietnamese, 134–135; Soup, wonton dumpling, with oriental chives, 78

Chinese leek: Pea Shoots with Crab Sauce, 147

Cilantro (coriander): Burritos, bean, 117; Chayote sauté with chilies, 158; Cheesecake, bell pepper, 91; Curry, golden chicken, 151; Curry, Thai red vegetable, 120; Eggplant, spicy, 182; Gazpacho, golden, 77; Herb blend, Asian, 23; Huevos rancheros, 107; Nachos, Technicolor, 130; Pizza, Mexican-style, with cilantro, 129; Pork stew with purslane, 139; Quesadillas, 128; Salad, cool white, 66; Salad, Oriana's cabbage, 51; Salad rolls, Vietnamese, 134–135; Salad, spicy and sour squid, 53; Salsa verde (tomatillo salsa), 37; Soup, fancy carrot and onion, 87; Soup, Thai chicken, 81; Soup, tortilla, 84; Soup, wonton dumpling with oriental chives, 78; Stir-fry, bitter melon with beef, 146; Stir-fry, carrot and garlic, 169; Stir-fry, pickled mustard with pork, 153; Stir-fry, shishito pepper and eggplant, 148; Squash blossoms, deep-fried, 92; Tacos, kaleidoscope, 118; Vinaigrette, Asian, 25

Vietnamese (rau ram): Salad, Henry's, with Vietnamese coriander, 62; Salad rolls, Vietnamese, 134–135

Coriander: see Cilantro

Corn: Chili, garden, 141; Chowder, summer squash and corn, 83; Esquites (spicy corn kernels), 99; Peppers, stuffed, 122; Pudding, corn, 167; Succotash, 161; Tacos, kaleidoscope, 118

Cucumber: Gazpacho, golden, 77

Cumin: Beans, refried, 34; Cheesecake, bell pepper, 91; Chili, black bean and chicken, 141; Chili, garden, 141; Curry, golden chicken, 151; Curry, Thai red vegetable, 120; Tex-Mex barbecue herb blend, hot, 24; Peppers, stuffed, 122; Pizza, Mexican-style, with cilantro, 129;

Ribs, babyback, with ancho chilies, 155; Sandwiches, pork shoulder, 136–137; Salad, cool white, 66; Soup, roasted pimiento, cream of, 74; Tacos, kaleidoscope, 118

Daikon: Curry, Thai red vegetable, 120; Daikon, pickled, and carrots, 30; Tempura, vegetable, 101

Dandelion greens: Soup, spring vegetable, with dumplings, 85

Dill: Flower canapés, 88; Herb blend, fresh flavor, 23; Salad, basic garden, 43; Soup, fancy carrot and onion, 87; Strudel, spinach feta, 103; Summer vegetables, Grandma Alice's, 159; Vegetable marinade, 25

Eggplant: Eggplant, spicy, 182; Pain bagna (French-style sandwich), 115; Stir-fry, shishito pepper and eggplant, 148; Tempura, vegetable, 101; Vegetables, barbecued, 177

Endive, Belgian: Belgian endive, braised, 161; Greens, hearty, with pears, 58; Salad, basic garden, 43; Salad, endive, with oranges and pistachios, 57; Salad, mesclun, 43

Fennel: Herbes de Provence, 24; Herbes de Provence à la Bouterin, 24; Potage de rouge vif d'etampes (pumpkin soup), 79; Rice, fennel, with pistachios, 131; Salad, fennel, with red peppers, 63; Vegetable marinade, 25; Vinaigrette, basic low-cal, 28

Florence: Pork, roast, with fennel stuffing, 155; Rice, fennel, with pistachios, 131

Figs: Fig Needhams (cookies), 195; Radicchio and mâche with figs and hazelnuts, 56

Flowers, edible: Butter, chive blossom, 29; Butter, nasturtium, 29; Flower canapés, 88; Flowers, candied, 193; Honey, rose petal, 38; Jelly, rose-scented geranium apple, 38–39; Omelet, squash blossom, 106; Salad, basic garden, 43; Salad, flower confetti, 46; Salad, garden bouquet, 46; Salad, Jody's sprout, 54; Salad, riot of color, 48; Salad, tangy, with roasted garlic dressing, 59; Salad, wild party, 45; Shortbread, lavender, 199; Squash blossoms, deep-fried, 92; Sugar, lavender, 38; Zucchini blossoms, stuffed, 99

Garlic: Beans, Italian-style, 171; Beans, refried, 34; Bean sprouts, spicy, 180; Broccoli raab, classic, 182; Chayote sauté with chilies, 158; Chili, black bean and chicken, 141; Chili, garden, 141; Curry, golden chicken, 151; Curry, Thai red vegetable, 120; Fettuccine with fresh marinara sauce, 114; Gado-gado, 121; Gazpacho, golden, 77; Gremolata (herb blend), 22; Gumbo, classic, 142; Huevos rancheros, 107; Lamb, gardener's spring, 137; Lasagna, roasted pepper, 125; Mole verde (green mole), 37; Mozzarella marinated with garlic, 97; Nachos, Technicolor, 130; Omelet, squash